USBORNE
WORLD KITCHEN CELEBRATIONS

Abigail Wheatley

ILLUSTRATED BY
Chaaya Prabhat

U.S. RECIPE CONSULTANT
Monita Buchwald

DESIGNED BY
Katie Goldwren

DIVERSITY CONSULTANTS
Show Racism the Red Card

USBORNE QUICKLINKS

Scan the code for links to websites where you can see how special occasions are celebrated around the world, watch how-to videos about basic cooking skills and discover fascinating facts about food, or go to usborne.com/Quicklinks and type in the title of this book.

You can also download some of the recipes in this book at Usborne Quicklinks, including guidance on how to make them vegan, dairy-free, egg-free, gluten-free and nut-free (or any combination of these.)

Usborne Publishing is not responsible for the content of external websites. Children should be supervised online. Please follow the online safety guidelines at usborne.com/Quicklinks

THANK YOU!

A huge thank you to all the families who made this book possible by contributing their stories and recipes.

CONTENTS

4   Getting started
6   Cooking basics
8   Recipe map
10 Carly's St. David's Day cakes
12 Jonathan's Halloween cookies
14 Celebration cakes
16 Giorgia's no-bake birthday cake
17 Arthur's Passover charoset
18 Lara's Twelfth Night cake
20 Batoul's family-time salad
22 Celebration fruits & vegetables
24 Tomoko's Girls' Day sushi
26 Elliya's Barbados Day conkies
28 Yve's Christmas Eve salad
30 Joanna's Day of the Dead bread
32 Celebration sweets
34 Araceli's Palm Sunday toast
36 Chloé's New Year dumplings
38 Oliver & Fran's ANZAC biscuits

40 Celebration drinks
42 Marilia's pool party limeade
43 Pinta's rice-festival pancakes
44 Paula's Shrovetide buns
46 Ben & Ethan's Thanksgiving tarts
48 Ishaque's Ramadan fritters
50 Celebration herbs & spices
52 Tara's celebration cake
54 Omoiho's party rice
56 Jaxon's New Year pie
58 Swapping ingredients
62 Index
64 Thanks and acknowledgements

GETTING STARTED

This book is full of delicious recipes contributed by families from all around the world. Their recipes are simple enough for beginner cooks and use widely-available ingredients, and equipment you should be able to find at home.

BEFORE YOU START

Read through the recipe to check you have all the ingredients and equipment you need. Wash your hands – then you're ready to go.

SERVING SIZES

The recipes in this book are for four people as a light meal or side dish, unless they say otherwise. If you want to make more, double all the ingredients. If you want to make less, halve them.

FOOD PREFERENCES & ALLERGIES

All of the recipes in this book are vegetarian and can also be made nut-free, gluten-free, egg-free, dairy-free, vegan, or almost any combination of these. For instructions, look for the "Variations" sign on the recipe pages, and on pages 58-61 at the end of the book.

A PINCH OF SALT

A pinch is the amount you can pick up between your thumb and your index finger. Some recipes include a pinch of salt. Others don't, as there's enough salt in other ingredients, such as soy sauce or cheese.

MEASURING

It's a good idea to measure ingredients accurately, especially when you're baking cakes or cookies. Small amounts are measured with measuring spoons. The ingredients should lie level with the top of the spoon.

ASK FOR HELP

Before you use new equipment, or if you're trying out something new, make sure you know what you're doing. If in doubt, ask someone with cooking experience to help you.

HANDLING PANS

Don't leave pan handles hanging over the front of the stove – turn them to the side, so you don't knock them off. Move hot pans carefully, so you don't spill the contents.

USING AN OVEN

Cook things on the middle shelf of the oven. Arrange the shelves before you turn on the oven. Some ovens may cook things more quickly or slowly than the recipe says. Set a timer to remind you when to take out your food.

OEVN MITTS

Food and equipment can get very hot. Protect your hands with oven mitts, especially when you're getting things in and out of the oven.

KEEP WATCH

Don't leave the kitchen while you've got anything cooking on the stove. Make sure you remember to turn off the heat when you've finished.

CLEAN UP

It's a good idea to wipe up any spills on the floor as you go, so you don't slip. If you keep the kitchen fairly tidy as you cook, it makes it easier to keep track of where you're up to, and helps when it comes to cleaning up afterwards.

CHOP SAFELY

When you're cutting with a sharp knife, use a cutting board to stop food from slipping. The recipe will tell you the safest way to chop things – or look at pages 6-7 for instructions on how to prepare some common ingredients.

COOKING BASICS

On these pages you'll find tips and techniques showing you how to do some common tasks mentioned in the recipes in this book. You can also watch how-to videos of all these techniques online – just follow the links on page 2 of this book.

PREPARING ONIONS

1. Cut off the top and root, and peel off the papery skin. Cut the onion in half.

2. Put each half flat side down and cut into thin slices.

3. Cut each slice into tiny pieces.

PREPARING GARLIC

1. Peel off the papery skin.

2. Crush the garlic in a garlic press.

WHIPPING CREAM

1. Pour the cream into a large bowl. If you're using a whisk, move it around and around in the cream very quickly.

2. If you're using an electric mixer, turn it to cream-whipping speed.

3. Lift up the whisk or mixer. The cream should stand up in a floppy point. If you whisk too much, the cream will become hard.

PREPARING POTATOES

1. Scrub the potatoes under cold running water.

2. Cut out any spots using a sharp knife.

CRACKING EGGS

1. Crack the egg sharply on the edge of a cup.

2. Push your thumbs into the crack and pull the shell apart.

3. Let the yolk and white slide gently out.

PREPARING BELL PEPPERS

1. Press with your thumbs on either side of the stalk, until it pops in.

2. Tear the pepper apart. Throw away the stalk, seeds and white parts.

PREPARING APPLES

1. Cut each apple in half. Put the halves flat side down and cut in half again.

2. To remove the cores, cut away from you, at a slant, to halfway under the core.

3. Turn the piece around and make another cut in the same way.

GREASING PANS

1. Dip a paper towel in some butter. Wipe it around inside the pan.

LINING SHALLOW PANS OR SHEETS

1. Put the pan or sheet on parchment paper and trace around it.

2. Snip out the shape, cutting just inside the line.

3. Put the shape in the bottom of the pan or sheet.

LINING DEEP PANS OR CONTAINERS

1. Put the pan on parchment paper like this. Trace around it, then cut across the whole strip.

2. Rotate the pan like this, put it on more parchment paper, trace around it and cut across the strip.

3. Put the thin strip in the bottom of the pan with its ends sticking up. Place the wide strip on top.

4. For a square container, the strips are the same width. Put one on top of the other.

I love making these crisp, frosted cookies with my sister for Halloween – though they're great for any special occasion.

My family loves making these delicately spiced cakes for St. David's day, when we celebrate everything Welsh.

NORTH AMERICA

Yve's Christmas Eve salad, p28
GERMANY

Carly's St. David's Day cakes, p10
WALES

Lara's Twelfth Night cake, p18
FRANCE

Ben & Ethan's Thanksgiving tarts, p46
CANADA

Jonathan's Halloween cookies, p12
USA

Araceli's Palm Sunday toast, p34
SPAIN

Giorgia's no-bake birthday cake, p16
ITALY

Joanna's Day of the Dead bread, p30
MEXICO

Elliya's Barbados Day conkies, p26
BARBADOS

AFRICA

My rich bread is for Day of the Dead (Dia de los Muertos) when Mexicans celebrate memories of their loved ones.

Tara's celebration cake, p52
GUYANA

SOUTH AMERICA

Omoiho's party rice, p54
NIGERIA

Arthur's Passover charoset, p17

Marilia's pool party limeade, p42
BRAZIL

I help my Nanny make this moist, dark fruit cake for all kinds of celebrations – from weddings to birthdays!

My Granny and I make this sweet paste for Passover – a Jewish religious festival. The recipe is not from one place. Jewish people have moved around the world for centuries, taking recipes with them. This happens with recipes from other traditions too.

8

RECIPE MAP

All the recipes in this book were sent in by families from around the world. This map shows you where the recipes are from.

EUROPE

ASIA

Paula's Shrovetide buns, p44
FINLAND

Jaxon's New Year pie, p56
BULGARIA

I make these yummy fritters at Ramadan, an important season in the Islamic religion.

Ishaque's Ramadan fritters, p48
BANGLADESH

Chloé's New Year dumplings, p36
SOUTH KOREA

Tomoko's Girls' Day sushi, p24
JAPAN

My sushi rice scattered with toppings is a delicious treat for Girls' Day, when we arrange displays of beautiful dolls.

Batoul's family-time salad, p20
SUDAN

I love eating this dish with my family, just to savor our daily time together.

Pinta's rice-festival pancakes, p43
INDONESIA

AUSTRALIA & NEW ZEALAND

We make these sweet, chewy treats for ANZAC Day, to remember everyone who has served in wars and conflicts. We call them biscuits, but you might call them cookies.

Oliver & Fran's ANZAC biscuits, p38
NEW ZEALAND

9

CARLY'S ST. DAVID'S DAY CAKES

Hi, I'm Carly and I come from Wales. This recipe is for Welsh cakes – little flat, spiced cakes cooked using a flat, round pan such as a frying pan or griddle. When I was little, my family always cooked them on March 1st, the day of Wales's saint, Dewi Sant (St. David). To celebrate his day, people eat Welsh food, and children wear traditional Welsh clothes to school.

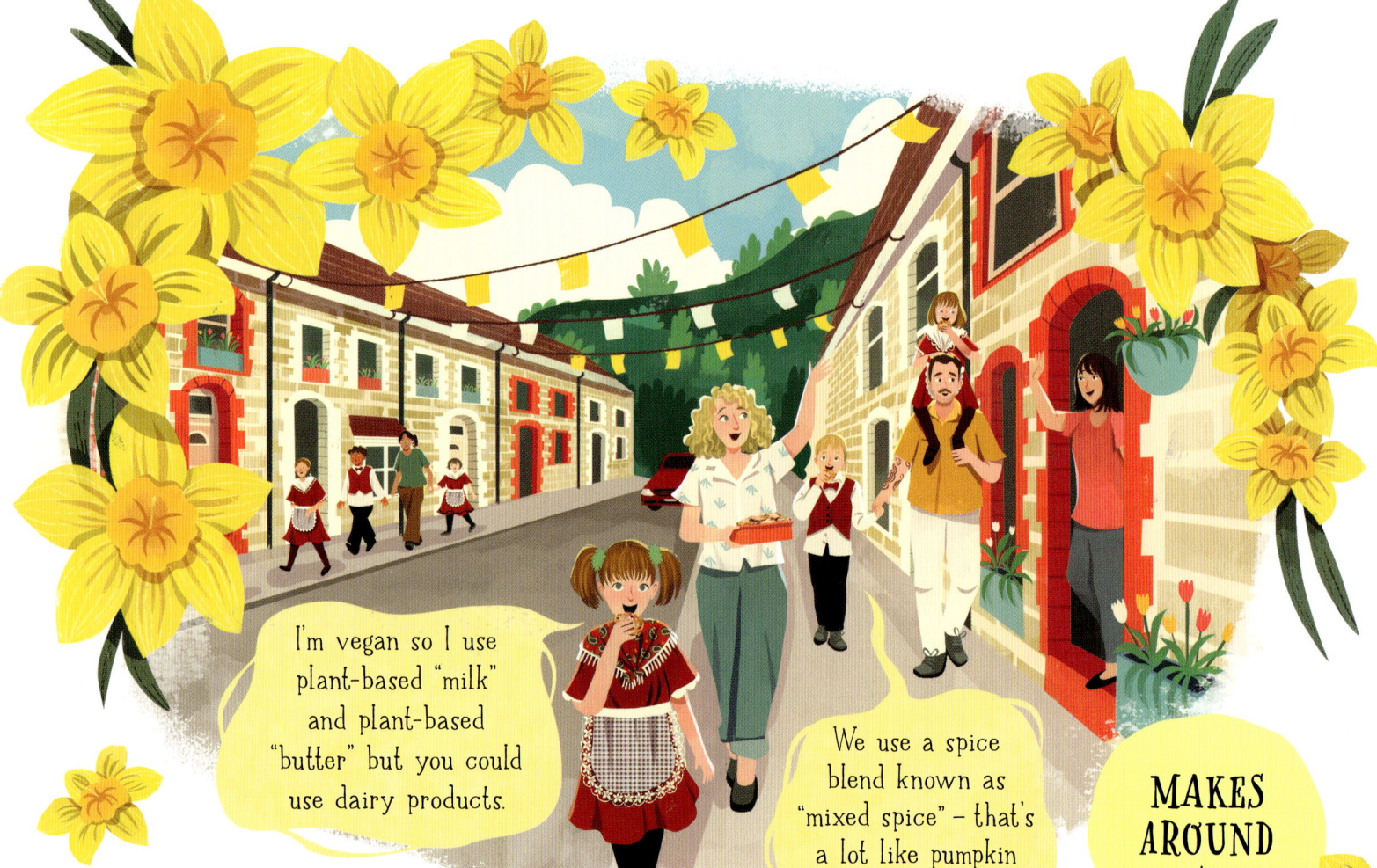

I'm vegan so I use plant-based "milk" and plant-based "butter" but you could use dairy products.

We use a spice blend known as "mixed spice" – that's a lot like pumpkin pie spice.

MAKES AROUND 12

INGREDIENTS

- 1 cup + 1½ tablespoons self-rising flour, plus a little extra for sprinkling
- ¾ teaspoon baking powder
- 1 teaspoon pumpkin pie spice
- 5 tablespoons cold plant-based "butter" from a block
- 2 tablespoons raisins or currants
- 3½ tablespoons sugar, plus a little extra for sprinkling
- 2 tablespoons plant-based "milk"
- cooking oil

You will also need a round or fluted round cutter around 3 inches across, and a frying pan or griddle, preferably non-stick.

1 Put the flour, baking powder and spice in big bowl.

Mix well.

2 Cut the "butter" into small chunks.

Put them in the bowl.

3 Pick up some "butter" and flour between your fingertips and thumbtips.

Squish and rub the butter and flour so they start to mix, letting them drop back into the bowl as you rub.

4 Keep on picking up and rubbing the mixture.

The lumps will get smaller. Stop when they look like small breadcrumbs.

5 Stir in the raisins or currants, and the sugar.

Then mix in the "milk" until it all sticks together.

6 Sprinkle a rolling pin and surface with flour. Put on the dough.

Roll until it's around as thick as a pencil.

7 Use the cutter to cut out lots of circles.

Squish the scraps together, roll them out and cut more circles, until the dough is used up.

8 Put the frying pan or griddle over medium heat and add 2 teaspoons oil. Put in 3 or 4 cakes.

Leave plenty of space between them, as this makes them easier to flip.

9 Cook for 2-3 minutes, then use a spatula to lift a corner.

If they're brown underneath, flip them over and cook for another 2 minutes. Then, lift onto a plate.

10 Repeat steps 8 and 9 again, until you have cooked all the cakes.

Sprinkle a little sugar on top. Eat them while they're still warm.

VARIATIONS

To make this recipe gluten-free, use gluten-free self-rising flour and gluten-free baking powder.

11

JONATHAN'S HALLOWEEN COOKIES

Hi there, my name is Jonathan. Every year at Halloween when I was growing up, me and my little sister Jenny made sugar cookies with our Mom, who comes from Virginia. We'd shape the dough with spooky-shaped cookie cutters, and frost the finished cookies ready for one of our legendary Halloween parties in our big, old barn – complete with piñatas, spooky food and, of course, creepy costumes.

We love decorating our cookies for Halloween, but this recipe is great for other celebrations too...

...you can use any shape of cookie cutters, and decorate your cookies any way you like.

THIS WAY TO THE PARTY

INGREDIENTS

For the cookies:
- ¼ cup (½ stick) softened butter or plant-based "butter" from a block
- ½ cup sugar
- 1 teaspoon vanilla extract
- 3 tablespoons milk or plant-based "milk"
- 1½ cups all-purpose flour
- ½ teaspoon baking powder

For the icing:
- 1 cup powdered sugar
- 4 teaspoons water
- a few drops vanilla extract
- a few drops food coloring
- little, round candies or edible eye decorations (optional)

You will also need cookie cutters and two baking sheets.

MAKES AROUND 20

1 Put the butter and sugar in a big bowl.

Mix them really hard with a spoon, until light and fluffy.

2 Stir in the vanilla and milk. Put a strainer or sifter over the bowl. Add the flour and baking powder.

Tap until they fall through. Mix until it clings together in a lump.

3 Take two large sheets of parchment paper. Put the dough on one sheet and cover it with the other.

Roll until the dough is almost as thick as a pencil.

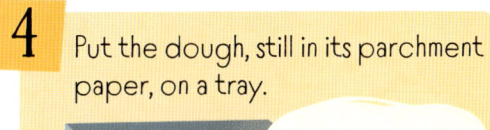

4 Put the dough, still in its parchment paper, on a tray.

Refrigerate for 15 minutes.

5 Next, heat the oven to 350°F.

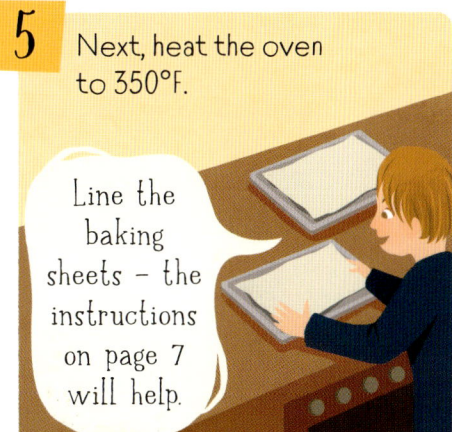

Line the baking sheets – the instructions on page 7 will help.

6 Then, put the dough on a work surface and peel off the top sheet of paper.

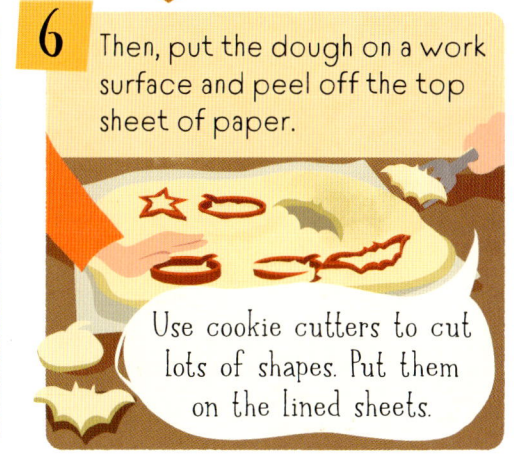

Use cookie cutters to cut lots of shapes. Put them on the lined sheets.

7 Squish the scraps of dough together, then roll them out between the sheets of paper again.

Cut more shapes, then squish, roll and cut again, until the dough is used up.

8 Bake for 10 minutes, or until they are just turning golden-brown at the edges.

Leave them on the sheets to cool completely.

9 For the icing, mix the powdered sugar, water and vanilla in a medium bowl.

Divide the mixture between small bowls. Stir a few drops of food coloring into each.

10 Spread icing on the cookies. Press on candies for eyes.

Enjoy! Or leave for a few hours if you want the icing to set firm.

VARIATIONS

To make this recipe gluten-free, use gluten-free flour and gluten-free baking powder.

To make it vegan or dairy-free, use plant-based "butter" and plant-based "milk."

CELEBRATION CAKES

From birthday cakes to wedding cakes and beyond – all around the world, people love sharing cakes as part of many different celebrations.

GHEVAR is a sweet, fried cake with a honeycomb-like texture. It originates from Rajasthan in northwestern India. People cook it for the festival of Teej, to welcome the rainy season, and also for Raksha Bandhan, a celebration of brothers and sisters.

SNOWSKIN MOONCAKES are popular in China, Singapore, Malaysia and Indonesia. They're enjoyed during the Moon Festival, held in mid-autumn. The outsides are made from a type of rice flour, with sweet fillings.

Turn to page 46 for an autumnal recipe from Canada.

BUCHE DE NOEL, or **YULE LOG**, is a log-shaped chocolate cake enjoyed at Christmas in France, Belgium, Switzerland and parts of Canada. It's often topped with sugary leaf or mushroom decorations, to make it look like a snowy forest log.

14

A Greek cake, **FANOUROPITA**, is made with flour, sugar, olive oil and orange juice. People bake the cake on August 27th in honor of Saint Fanourios, who's believed to help find lost things.

SARAWAK LAYER CAKE is a colorful cake made of lots of layers, which is a favorite in Malaysia. People often enjoy it for special occasions such as Eid, Christmas, birthdays or weddings.

PRINSESSTARTA, or Princess Cake, is one of Sweden's most popular cakes. It's made from layers of sponge, whipped cream and sometimes jam, and topped with marzipan. It's very popular for birthday parties.

You'll find an Italian Birthday cake recipe on page 16.

A cake called **PARKIN** is enjoyed in the North of England for Bonfire Night on November 5th – when people gather for fireworks and bonfires. Parkin is sweet and sticky, made using oats and often flavored with ginger.

15

GIORGIA'S NO-BAKE BIRTHDAY CAKE

Ciao! I'm Giorgia and I'm from Italy. When I was small, for my birthdays, my Dad and I made a simple cake using melted chocolate and graham crackers rolled into a sausage shape. We call it "salame di cioccolato" or chocolate salami.

INGREDIENTS

- 5oz semi-sweet or milk chocolate
- 5 tablespoons butter
- ¼ cup sugar
- 4 tablespoons unsweetened cocoa powder
- 2 tablespoons milk
- 12 graham crackers or vanilla wafers
- icing sugar for dusting

For a rich taste, we use semi-sweet chocolate AND cocoa powder, but you can use milk chocolate and leave out the cocoa.

1 Break the chocolate into a heatproof bowl. Add the butter and sugar. Put the bowl over a saucepan half full of water, over medium heat.

When the water bubbles, turn off the heat. Stir until melted.

2 Carefully remove the bowl from the saucepan. Stir in the cocoa powder and milk.

Break the crackers or wafers into small pieces into the bowl. Stir well.

3 Cut a big piece of parchment paper. Put the mixture on it. Shape it into a long sausage.

Roll the paper up around it. Twist the ends. Refrigerate for 2 hours.

4 Unwrap it. Sift on the powdered sugar.

Roll to coat it all over. Cut into slices before eating.

VARIATIONS

To make this recipe gluten-free, dairy-free or vegan, follow the instructions on page 58.

ARTHUR'S PASSOVER CHAROSET

Hello, my name is Arthur. My family is Jewish. Every year we celebrate Passover, one of the most important festivals in our religion, Judaism. We get together to say prayers and eat special foods including charoset – a sweet paste made from fruit and nuts. I love rolling this mixture into little balls with my Granny, ready for the Passover meal.

INGREDIENTS

- 1 medium-sized sweet apple
- 1 cup dried fruit such as raisins, stoned dates, apricots or a mixture
- ⅔ cup almond flour (leave this out if anyone is allergic to nuts – see "Variations" below)
- a pinch ground cinnamon
- 1 tablespoon powdered sugar
- 1 little gem lettuce

We serve our charoset balls in lettuce leaves, but you can eat them on their own if you prefer.

1 Shred the apple. Stop when you get near the core.

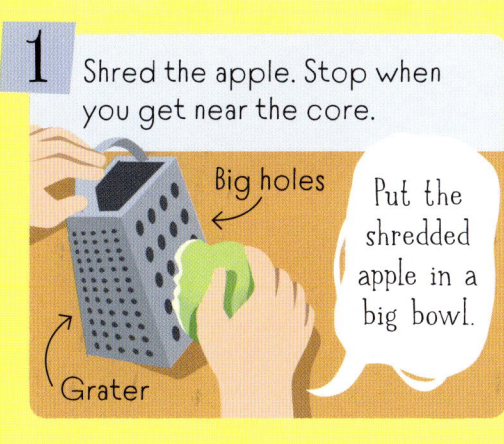

Put the shredded apple in a big bowl.

Big holes — Grater

2 If you're using raisins, put them in a cup and snip them into tiny pieces.

If you're using dates or dried apricots, snip them into tiny pieces, too.

Put them all in the bowl. Add the almond flour, cinnamon and powdered sugar. Mix well.

3 Use your hands to squash and roll the mixture into bite-size balls.

4 Carefully separate the leaves from the lettuce.

Nestle each ball on a lettuce leaf to serve.

VARIATIONS

To make this recipe nut-free, follow the instructions on page 58.

17

LARA'S TWELFTH NIGHT CAKE

Hi! I'm Lara and my family's from France. My recipe is for a delicious pastry dessert my Grand-Mère (Grandmother) used to make when I was little, for Twelfth Night – the 12th day after Christmas. It's called 'galette des rois' (cake of the kings) after three kings who feature in the story of Christmas. It has a sweet filling containing almond flour, but you can make a nut-free version too.

Traditionally, a bean or china ornament is hidden in the galette – if you find it, you're king for the day and wear a paper crown.

This recipe contains nuts – but there's a nut-free version on page 58.

INGREDIENTS

- a little flour for sprinkling
- 1 store-bought frozen puff pastry sheet
- ¼ cup (½ stick) butter
- ⅓ cup sugar
- 1 large egg
- 1 teaspoon vanilla extract
- 1 cup + 3 tablespoons almond flour
- a little milk for brushing

You will also need a large baking tray and a round plate that's around 9 inches across.

TIP

Before you start, leave the pastry and butter at room temperature for 30 minutes.

1 Heat the oven to 400°F.

Line the tray with parchment paper – the instructions on page 7 will help you.

2 Dust a surface and rolling pin with flour. Unroll the pastry.

Put on the plate. Cut around it like this. Put the pastry circle aside.

3 Gently pile up the scraps of pastry and roll them out.

Use the plate to cut another circle. Put it on the tray.

4 Put the butter and sugar in a big bowl. Mix with a wooden spoon, then beat really hard until soft and pale.

5 Add the egg and beat hard again to mix it in.

Add the vanilla and almond flour. Mix them in gently. This is your filling.

6 Spoon the filling over the pastry on the tray.

Leave a 1 inch gap around the edge.

7 Wet a finger and run it all around the edge of the pastry to make it damp.

Lift the other circle of pastry on top.

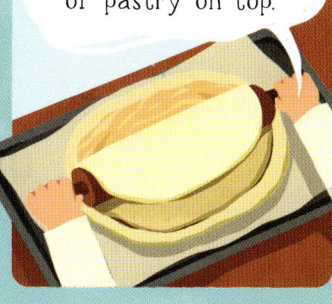

8 Dip a fork in flour, then press it onto the edge of the pastry, to seal it.

Do this again and again all around the pastry to seal it really well.

9 Poke a hole in the top of the pastry. Then, gently mark a pattern on the surface of the pastry using a knife.

Then brush a little milk over the top.

10 Bake for 30 minutes, until risen and golden. Leave to cool on the tray for 20 minutes.

Eat warm or cold, cut into slices.

VARIATIONS

To make this recipe nut-free, gluten-free, egg-free, dairy-free or vegan, see page 58 for instructions.

BATOUL'S FAMILY-TIME SALAD

Hello, my name is Batoul and I come from Sudan. Spending time with family, and eating together, is very important in Sudan. When I was young, as soon as my seven sisters and I got home from school, we would all start preparing a family meal together. Each child had a task – one cleaned, one made tea, another set the table, while my mother Sitana cooked. Often she made this spicy eggplant dish – we call it a salad but to you it might seem more like a dip.

We fry our eggplant, but it may be easier for you to bake it.

This dish is spicy! Leave out the chili if you prefer.

This recipe contains peanuts – but in "Variations" you can see how to swap in other ingredients.

1 Cut the eggplant into slices as thick as your finger. Cut the slices into strips as wide as your finger.

Then, cut the strips into cubes.

2 To fry the eggplant, put the pan over medium heat and add 3 tablespoons of the oil. Add the eggplant and salt.

Cook, stirring, for 10 minutes until soft and golden. Put in a bowl to cool. Skip to step 4.

3 To bake the eggplant, heat the oven to 400°F. Mix the eggplant, 3 tablespoons of the oil and the salt on a baking sheet.

Put in the oven for 25 minutes, until soft and golden. Set aside to cool.

4 Peel the papery skin off the onion and garlic. Cut the onion into small pieces and crush the garlic.

The instructions on page 6 will help you.

5 Cut the tomato into slices, then into small pieces.

6 Cut the top off the chili, then cut the rest into small pieces.

INGREDIENTS

- 1 medium eggplant
- 4 tablespoons cooking oil
- a pinch salt
- ½ onion, or 1 small onion
- 3 cloves garlic
- 1 medium tomato
- 1 green chili pepper (optional)
- 1 lemon
- 1 tablespoon of tomato paste
- 2 tablespoons smooth peanut butter
- 1 pinch chili powder (optional)
- ⅓ cup water

You will also need a large pan, preferably non-stick.

TIP
If you can, use peanut butter just made from peanuts with nothing else added.

7 Cut the lemon in half. Squeeze the juice from one half.

You don't need the other half.

← Citrus squeezer

8 Put the pan over medium heat. Add the remaining tablespoon of oil and the onion.

Cook for 2 minutes until soft.

9 Stir in the garlic. Cook for a minute. Then mix in the tomato paste, chopped tomato and chili.

Cook for 2 minutes, stirring often.

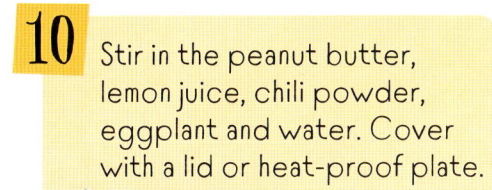

10 Stir in the peanut butter, lemon juice, chili powder, eggplant and water. Cover with a lid or heat-proof plate.

Leave to cook for 5 more minutes.

VARIATIONS

To make this recipe peanut-free, replace the peanut butter with another type of nut butter such as almond.

To make it peanut-free and nut-free, replace the peanut butter with tahini (sesame seed paste) or nut-free "peanut butter."

CELEBRATION FRUITS & VEGETABLES

Our world is home to an amazing variety of fruits and vegetables. Many of them are key ingredients in celebratory foods – while others have become so popular that they even have their own fesitvals.

In Switzerland, **ONIONS** are bought, eaten and celebrated every November at Zibelemärit (meaning 'onion market') in the town of Bern. It's said to have been taking place for more than 600 years. Onion pie and onion soup are popular dishes.

UBE is a yam or sweet potato with a bright purple middle. In the Philippines, ube is used to make celebration cakes – because of their bright color, they're much loved at all celebrations and parties.

APPLES and **POMEGRANATES** are part of a special meal eaten for Rosh Hashanah, a New Year festival celebrated in September or October in the Jewish religion. People often dip the apples in honey, wishing for a sweet New Year, and eat the many seeds from the pomegranates hoping for a year full of many good things.

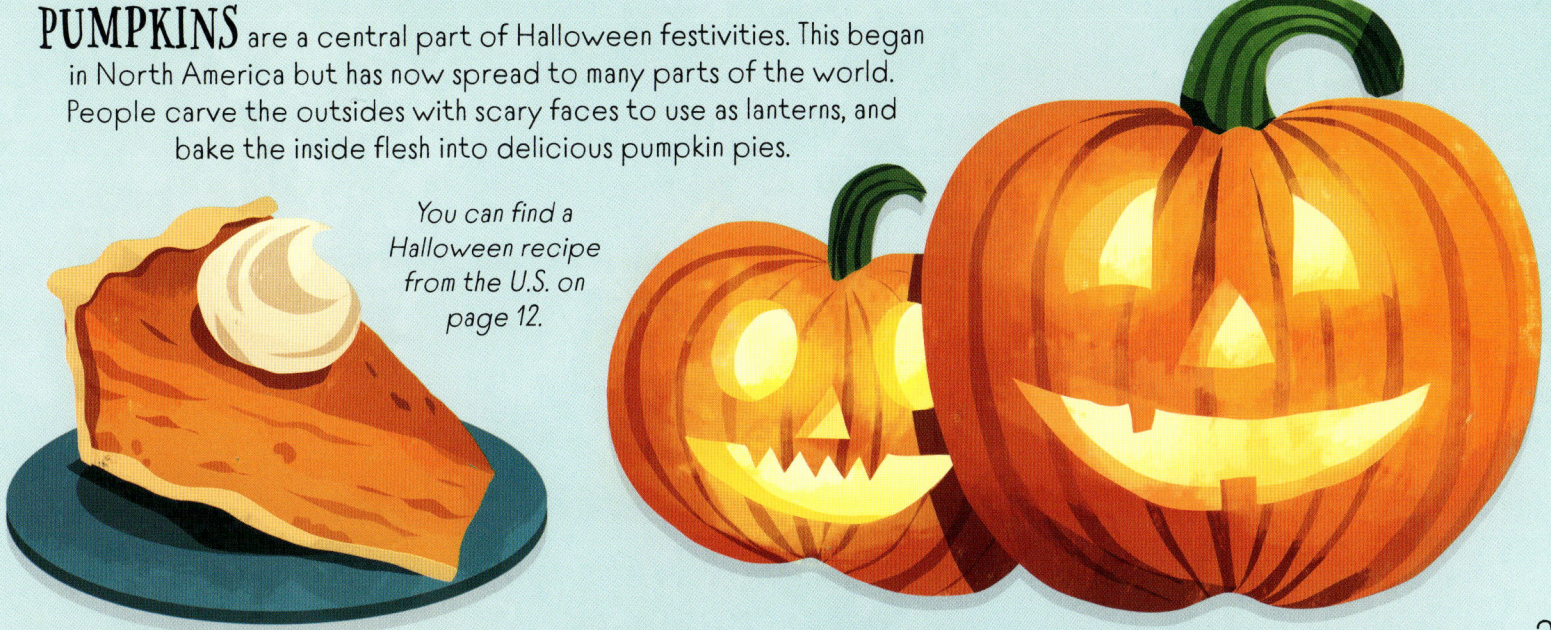

PINEAPPLES are important for the festival of Lunar New Year in parts of China, Singapore, Malaysia and the Philippines. People hang pineapple decorations for luck, and eat pineapple tarts and sweet treats.

Sweet, soft **DATES** are enjoyed during Ramadan – a month when people of the Muslim religion don't eat or drink anything during daylight. As the Sun sets, people often share dates and a glass of tea, before eating a meal together.

You can find a Ramadan recipe for eggplant fritters on page 48.

PUMPKINS are a central part of Halloween festivities. This began in North America but has now spread to many parts of the world. People carve the outsides with scary faces to use as lanterns, and bake the inside flesh into delicious pumpkin pies.

You can find a Halloween recipe from the U.S. on page 12.

23

TOMOKO'S GIRLS' DAY SUSHI

Hello, my name is Tomoko and I'm from Japan. Every March when I was growing up, I celebrated Hinamatsuri, or Girls' Day, with my Okaasan (Mom) and my sister Keiko. We set up a display of traditional dolls in our home, unwrapping their tiny, beautiful accessories from tissue paper. Then we ate chirashizushi, or scattered sushi – a bowl of sushi rice scattered with vegetables and other colorful toppings.

As well as for Girls' Day, we also eat chirashizushi on other happy occasions such as parties.

Every family has a different chirashizushi recipe, but this is ours.

INGREDIENTS

- 1¼ cups sushi rice
- 1½ cups water
- 3 tablespoons rice vinegar or white wine vinegar
- 2 tablespoons sugar
- a little table salt
- ½ cup sugar snap peas (optional)
- 3 large eggs
- cooking oil
- 8 cherry tomatoes
- half an English cucumber
- 2 tablespoons sesame seeds (optional)

24

1 Rinse the rice in a strainer under cold water until the water that runs out is clear, not cloudy.

Put in a pot. Add the 1½ cups water. Set aside for 30 minutes.

2 Put the vinegar, sugar and a pinch of salt into a small pot, over medium heat.

Stir until the sugar disappears. Leave to cool.

3 Half fill a pot with water. Put over medium heat. When the water bubbles, add the snap peas.

Cook for 1 minute, then drain and rinse in cold water.

4 Crack an egg into a cup (see page 6). Beat to mix the yolk and white.

Put a little oil in a small frying pan over medium heat.

5 After one minute, pour in the egg.

Tilt the pan to spread out the egg. Cook for 2 minutes, until the egg all looks solid. Slide onto a plate.

6 Repeat steps 4 and 5 again to make 2 more omelets.

When they're cool, fold them in half and cut into strips.

7 Cut the snap peas into small strips.

Cut the tomatoes into slices.

8 Cut the cucumber into quarters lengthways, then cut into small slices.

Put in a bowl. Mix in a pinch of salt. Set aside.

9 Cook the rice in a rice cooker, or put the rice pan over medium heat. Put on a lid.

Leave a small gap.

When the water bubbles, turn down the heat so the water is just bubbling. Cook for 10 minutes.

10 Turn off the heat. Leave for 10 minutes. Stir in the cooled vinegar mixture.

We fan our rice to cool it, but you can just leave it to cool. Then, put in a bowl.

11 Squeeze the cucumber to get rid of any water.

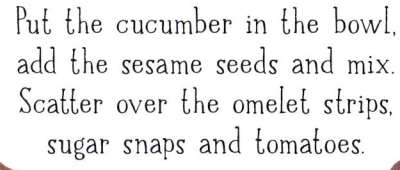

Put the cucumber in the bowl, add the sesame seeds and mix. Scatter over the omelet strips, sugar snaps and tomatoes.

VARIATIONS

You could stir some cooked broccoli, salmon or shrimp into the rice before you add the toppings.

To make this recipe egg-free and vegan, follow the instructions on page 59.

25

ELLIYA'S BARBADOS DAY CONKIES

Hi, I'm Elliya and I live on the Caribbean island of Barbados. My recipe is for conkies – a sweet treat of pumpkin, coconut and raisins. For centuries, conkies have been cooked here in November, and they're now part of celebrations for Barbados Independence Day, on November 30th. A dear friend, Gaulda, has helped my family make conkies for years – first she helped my Great Grandmother, then my Gran-Gran, my Auntie, and now it's me!

We wrap our conkies in banana leaves – but you can wrap yours in parchment paper.

INGREDIENTS

- 2 tablespoons unsweetened shredded coconut
- 3 tablespoons milk
- half of a small (6oz) sweet potato – or use a mixture of pumpkin or squash and sweet potato that adds up to this weight
- ¼ cup cornmeal, either coarse or fine
- 1 cup packed light brown sugar
- 1 tablespoon all-purpose flour
- 2 tablespoons raisins
- ½ teaspoon pumpkin pie spice
- a pinch ground nutmeg
- 4 tablespoons (½ stick) butter

MAKES 4

You will also need a steamer (or a metal strainer or colander) and a lidded pot to fit it.

1. Put the coconut and milk in a bowl. Set aside.

2. Use a peeler to peel the skin off the sweet potato, pumpkin or squash.

   Shred on the small holes of a grater or whiz up in a food processor.

   You need ¾ cup of the whizzed or shredded bits.

3. Put the shredded bits in a big bowl.

   Stir in the cornmeal, sugar, flour, raisins, pumpkin pie spice and nutmeg.

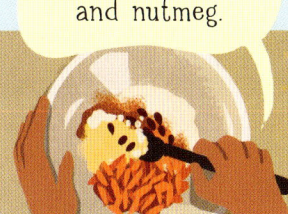

4. Put the butter in a small pot over gentle heat until it melts.

   Put the butter and the coconut and milk mixture in the big bowl. Mix well.

5. Cut four large squares of parchment paper.

   Divide the mixture between them.

6. Take one sheet. Pick up two opposite sides and line up the top edges.

   Fold them over around 1 inch from the top. Then keep folding over and over until you reach the mixture.

7. Take an open end and fold it under by around 1 inch. Keep folding under until you reach the mixture.

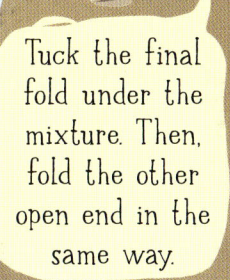

   Tuck the final fold under the mixture. Then, fold the other open end in the same way.

8. Repeat steps 6 and 7 with the remaining sheets, until all the conkies are wrapped.

   Put in the steamer, strainer or colander in one layer.

9. Put 2 inches of water in the lidded pot. Fit on the steamer, strainer or colander. Put on the lid.

   Put the pot over medium heat until the water bubbles, then turn the heat to low.

10. Cook for 20 minutes. Every few minutes, check there is still water in the pot – add more if it gets low.

    Take the steamer, strainer or colander out of the pot and leave everything to cool.

11. Unwrap and eat the conkies while they're still warm.

    They're also yummy cold!

VARIATIONS

To make this recipe gluten-free, dairy-free or vegan, see the instructions on page 59.

YVE'S CHRISTMAS EVE SALAD

Hi there, my name is Yve and I'm from Germany. This is a recipe that I helped my Mama cook when I was little – and she learned it from her Mama. It's a potato salad made with mayonnaise and crisp, sweet apple. We always made it for lunch on Christmas Eve. We prepared it slowly and lovingly, making our own mayo and cutting all the ingredients into tiny cubes – but you can use store-bought mayo, and not cut things so small.

We love to add sweet gherkins and hard boiled eggs to our potato salad – but you could leave them out.

Use pink apples if you can get them.

INGREDIENTS

- 1lb Yukon Gold or russet potatoes
- 2 large eggs (optional)
- 10 sweet gherkin pickles
- 1½ tablespoons liquid from the gherkin jar
- 1 sweet, pink apple
- 5 tablespoons mayonnaise
- a pinch salt and pepper

1 Prepare the potatoes – see page 6 for help. Then put the potatoes in a big pot. Add cold water to cover them.

2 Put a lid on the pot and put it over high heat, until the water bubbles. Leave a gap. Turn the heat to medium/low, so the water just bubbles. Cook for 10-15 minutes.

3 Poke a knife into a potato. If it feels soft, it's cooked. If not, cook for 5 minutes more, then test again. Drain the potatoes. Leave them to cool.

4 Meanwhile, half fill a small pot with water and put it over medium heat. Slotted spoon. When the water bubbles, carefully lower in the eggs.

5 Turn down the heat so the water bubbles gently. Cook for 9 minutes. Lift out the eggs and set them aside in a bowl of cold water.

6 Cut the sweet gherkins into small pieces around ½ inch across. Put them in a big bowl. Add the gherkin liquid.

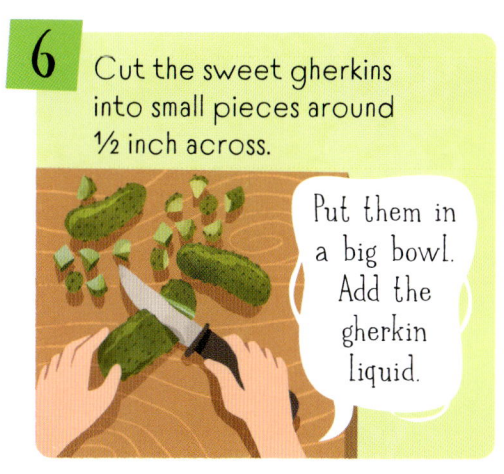

7 Cut out the cores from the apples – the instructions on page 7 will help you.

8 Then, cut the apple into cubes the same size as the gherkin pieces.

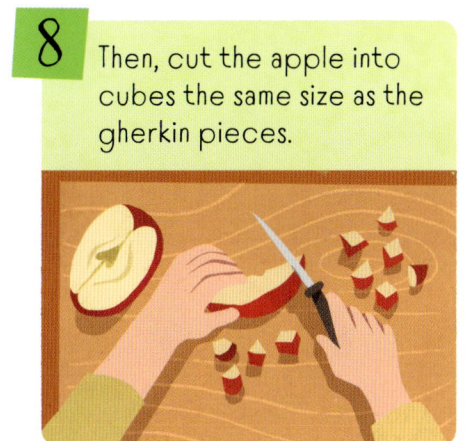

9 Cut the potatoes in half. Cut the halves into slices as wide as two fingers. Cut the slices into pieces as wide as one finger.

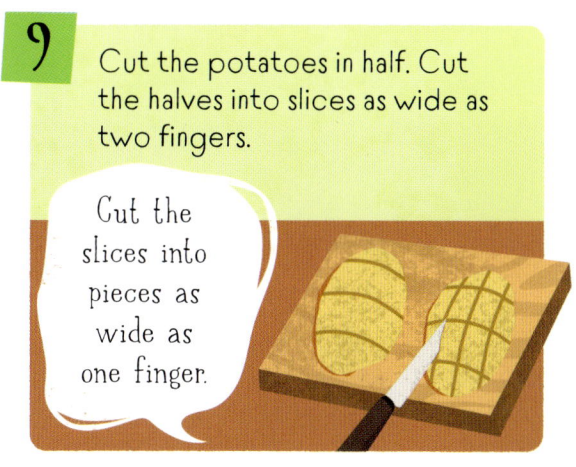

10 Put the gherkin, apple and potato pieces in a big bowl. Add the mayonnaise, salt and pepper. Mix gently.

11 Tap the egg shells on a cutting board, to crack them all over. Peel off the shells. Cut the eggs into cubes the same size as the apple and gherkin. Put them in the bowl.

VARIATIONS

To make this recipe egg-free or vegan, leave out the eggs and use plant-based "mayonnaise."

JOANNA'S DAY OF THE DEAD BREAD

Hi, I'm Joanna. My family's from Mexico. At the start of November, Mexicans celebrate Day of the Dead (Día de los Muertos) by sharing food and happy memories of loved ones who have died. I bake 'pan de muerto' (bread of the dead) with my big brother's girlfriend, Claudia. We put it on a decorated table with photos of our loved ones.

Most Mexicans buy pan de muerto, but it's fun to make it at home.

It takes 6 hours to make it the authentic way... but this recipe is much quicker and easier.

INGREDIENTS

- 1 orange
- 3 cups all-purpose flour, plus extra for sprinkling
- ¾ cup (1½ sticks) butter
- 3 teaspoons (1½ packets) fast-acting (instant) yeast
- 1 teaspoon orange flower water, or vanilla extract
- ¾ cup + 3 tablespoons milk

For the topping:
- 2 tablespoons butter
- 2 tablespoons sugar

TIP
Before you start, leave the butter at room temperature for one hour.

1. Line a big baking sheet – see page 7 for instructions.

   Grate the orange zest from the outside of the orange.

2. Put the zest, flour, butter, yeast and the orange flower water or vanilla in a big bowl.

3. Put the milk in a small pot over gentle heat. After 2 minutes, dip in the tip of a finger.

   It should just feel warm. Stir it into the flour mixture.

4. Sprinkle a surface with flour. Pour on the dough. If it's very sticky, sprinkle on extra flour.

   Push the dough away from you, using your knuckles or the heels of your hands.

5. Fold the dough in half towards you...

   ...then push it away again.

   Keep doing this for 5-10 minutes, or until the dough is smooth and springy.

6. Put the dough back in the bowl in a warm place (see page 44) for an hour, or until doubled in size.

   Plate

7. Then, knead the dough again (see above) for two minutes.

   Set aside a piece of dough the size of an apple. Pat the rest into a big ball. Put it on the baking sheet.

8. Divide the apple-sized piece into 3 equal pieces.

   Roll two of them into long rope shapes, and the other into a small ball.

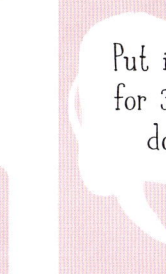

9. Arrange the long ropes in a cross on top of the big ball. Put the small ball on top.

   Put in a warm place for 30 minutes, until doubled in size.

10. Heat the oven to 350°F.

    Bake for 30-40 minutes, or until deep golden-brown.

11. For the topping, melt the butter in a small pot over gentle heat.

    Brush on the butter, then sprinkle on the sugar.

    Leave to cool on the sheet.

    Pastry brush

VARIATIONS

To make this recipe gluten-free, use gluten-free bread flour.

To make it dairy-free and vegan, use plant-based "butter" and plant-based "milk."

31

CELEBRATION SWEETS

In all corners of the globe, sweet treats are a way of celebrating. In some cultures they're left in temples as festive offerings. In others they're simply eaten and enjoyed.

FRUTTA MARTORANA
are small, fruit-shaped treats molded from colored almond paste. They originated in the Italian island of Sicily, where they are given to children to celebrate All Soul's Day on November 2nd.

EASTER EGGS,
especially chocolate eggs, are enjoyed across the world in the spring, to celebrate new life and the festival of Easter. Easter is a Christian festival, but Easter eggs have become so popular that now many people enjoy them.

To find a Spanish recipe for Easter time, turn to page 34.

KESAR PEDA
is a fudge made from milk flavored with spices – saffron and cardamom. It's one of many treats popular in India during Diwali, a festival of lights that's celebrated around September to November.

LOKUM, sometimes known as **TURKISH DELIGHT**, is a sugary candy that comes in many flavors such as rose, lemon and mint. It's very popular in Greece, Turkey, Iran and nearby countries, where it's shared at celebrations such as weddings.

PAÇOCA is a candy made from peanuts, sugar and honey. It originates from Brazil, and is especially eaten during Festas Juninas – a country summer festival that celebrates the end of the rainy season.

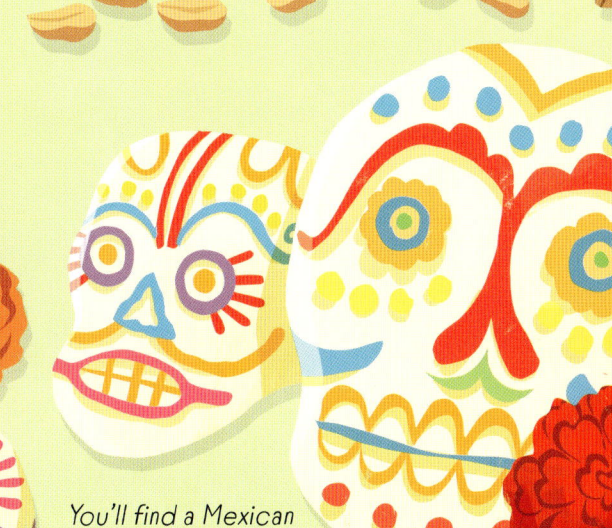

CALAVERAS, or **SUGAR SKULLS**, are popular in Mexico for Day of the Dead, or Día de los Muertos, celebrated around the start of November. The small skulls are made from sugar – or sometimes chocolate – but not all are made to be eaten. Some are used as decorations.

You'll find a Mexican recipe for Day of the Dead on page 30.

CANDY CANES may have been invented in Germany to keep children quiet during Christmas church services. For the last 150 years, they've been popular in the U.S. as Christmas treats and decorations, and this tradition has spread around the world.

There's a Christmas recipe from Germany on page 28.

ARACELI'S PALM SUNDAY TOAST

Hi, I'm Araceli and I'm from Spain. When I was small, I cooked this delicious toast with my sisters and our Mami (Mother) on Palm Sunday – a Christian holy day just before Easter. It's made from slices of bread that are cooked and dusted with sugar – we call them "torrijas." Each sister was in charge of one step in preparing the torrijas, while Mami did the cooking. We loved both making and eating them!

We use a type of white bread that comes in sticks. Where you live, it might be called a baguette.

This recipe works well with stale bread, around a day old – but fresh bread is ok too.

INGREDIENTS

- a small baguette – around 7oz
- ½ cup milk
- a little sugar
- ¼ teaspoon vanilla extract
- 1 large egg
- ½ teaspoon ground cinnamon
- 4 tablespoons cooking oil

MAKES AROUND 8 PIECES

You will also need a frying pan, preferably non-stick.

1 Cut the bread into diagonal slices around 1 inch thick.

Use the heels for something else.

2 Put the milk in a shallow bowl. Add 1 teaspoon sugar.

Add the vanilla. Stir well.

3 Crack the egg into a shallow bowl – the instructions on page 6 will help you.

Beat the yolk and white together.

Fork →

4 Mix the cinnamon and 2 tablespoons of sugar in a shallow bowl.

5 Put the frying pan over medium heat. Add 2 tablespoons of the oil.

6 Quickly dip a piece of bread into the milk. Flip it over to coat both sides.

Then quickly dip both sides in the egg in the same way.

7 Then, slide it carefully into the pan, like this.

Dip and slide half the slices of bread in the same way.

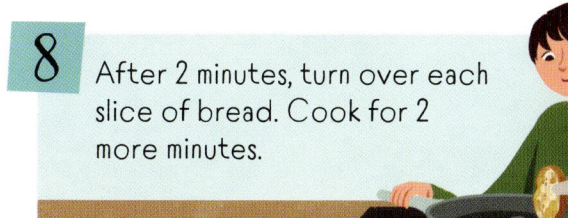

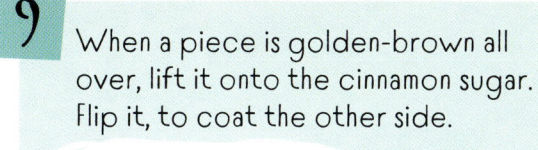

8 After 2 minutes, turn over each slice of bread. Cook for 2 more minutes.

9 When a piece is golden-brown all over, lift it onto the cinnamon sugar. Flip it, to coat the other side.

Put it on a serving plate, and cover with an upside-down plate.

10 Put another 2 tablespoons oil in the pan, then coat, cook and sugar the remaining torrijas.

Eat them while they're warm!

VARIATIONS

To make this recipe gluten-free, use gluten-free bread.

To make it dairy-free, use plant-based "milk."

To make it egg-free, replace the egg with 4 tablespoons cornstarch or chickpea flour, and 4 tablespoons water, whisked together in a shallow bowl.

To make it vegan, make it dairy-free and gluten-free following the instructions above.

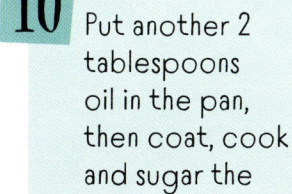

35

CHLOÉ'S NEW YEAR DUMPLINGS

Hi, I'm Chloé and my Eomma (Mom) is from South Korea. In January or February, we celebrate Seollal (or Lunar New Year) by wearing traditional clothes and spending time with family, cooking together and sharing delicious food. My Eomma has taught me to make these dumplings, which her family always eats at Seollal. They're filled with kimchi – a very popular Korean food.

At Seollal we eat these dumplings in soup, but they're also delicious eaten on their own.

Kimchi is spicy, but here it's mixed with a mild ingredient called tofu – so the dumplings are only a little spicy.

MAKES 6-8

INGREDIENTS

For the dumpling dough:
- ½ cup + 2 tablespoons all-purpose flour
- ½ cup water
- ½ teaspoon sesame oil
- a pinch table salt

For the filling:
- 2oz (scant ⅓ cup) bought kimchi
- 1½oz regular or firm tofu (¼ cup when crumbled)
- ½ teaspoon seasame oil

You will also need a round cookie cutter around 4 inches across, and a steamer (or a metal strainer or colander) and a lidded pan to fit it.

1 To make the dough, put the flour, water, oil and salt in a bowl. Mix, then use your hands to squish it into a smooth ball.

Wrap tightly in a big piece of parchment paper and set aside.

2 For the filling, drain the kimchi in a strainer over a sink.

Then put the kimchi in a cup and snip it into tiny bits.

Scissors

3 Crumble the tofu. Put it in the strainer with the chopped kimchi.

Press with a small plate, so any liquid drains away.

4 Put the kimchi and tofu in a bowl. Add the sesame oil.

Mix well. This is the filling.

5 Unwrap the dough. Put it on a surface sprinkled with flour.

Use the parchment paper to line the steamer.

6 Use a floured rolling pin to roll out the dough as thin as you can.

Cut lots of circles using the cutter. Put the scraps of dough aside.

7 Put a teaspoon of filling on each circle, then run a wet finger around the edge.

Fold each circle in half. Press the edges together all around, to seal.

8 Pinch the points of the semicircle together, like this.

Put the dumpling in the steamer.

9 Make more dumplings until the circles are used up. Then, roll out the dough scraps and make more circles.

Make more dumplings, until the dough is used up. Put them all in the steamer, in a single layer.

10 Put around 2 inches water in the pan. Fit in the steamer. Put on the lid.

Put it over a medium heat, until the water boils.

11 When the water boils, turn down the heat so it bubbles gently. Cook for 10 minutes.

Leave for 5 minutes, then carefully lift out the paper and dumplings. Enjoy warm.

VARIATIONS

To make this recipe gluten-free, replace the flour with gluten-free bread flour.

To make it sesame-free, use vegetable oil such as olive oil instead of the sesame oil.

OLIVER & FRAN'S ANZAC BISCUITS

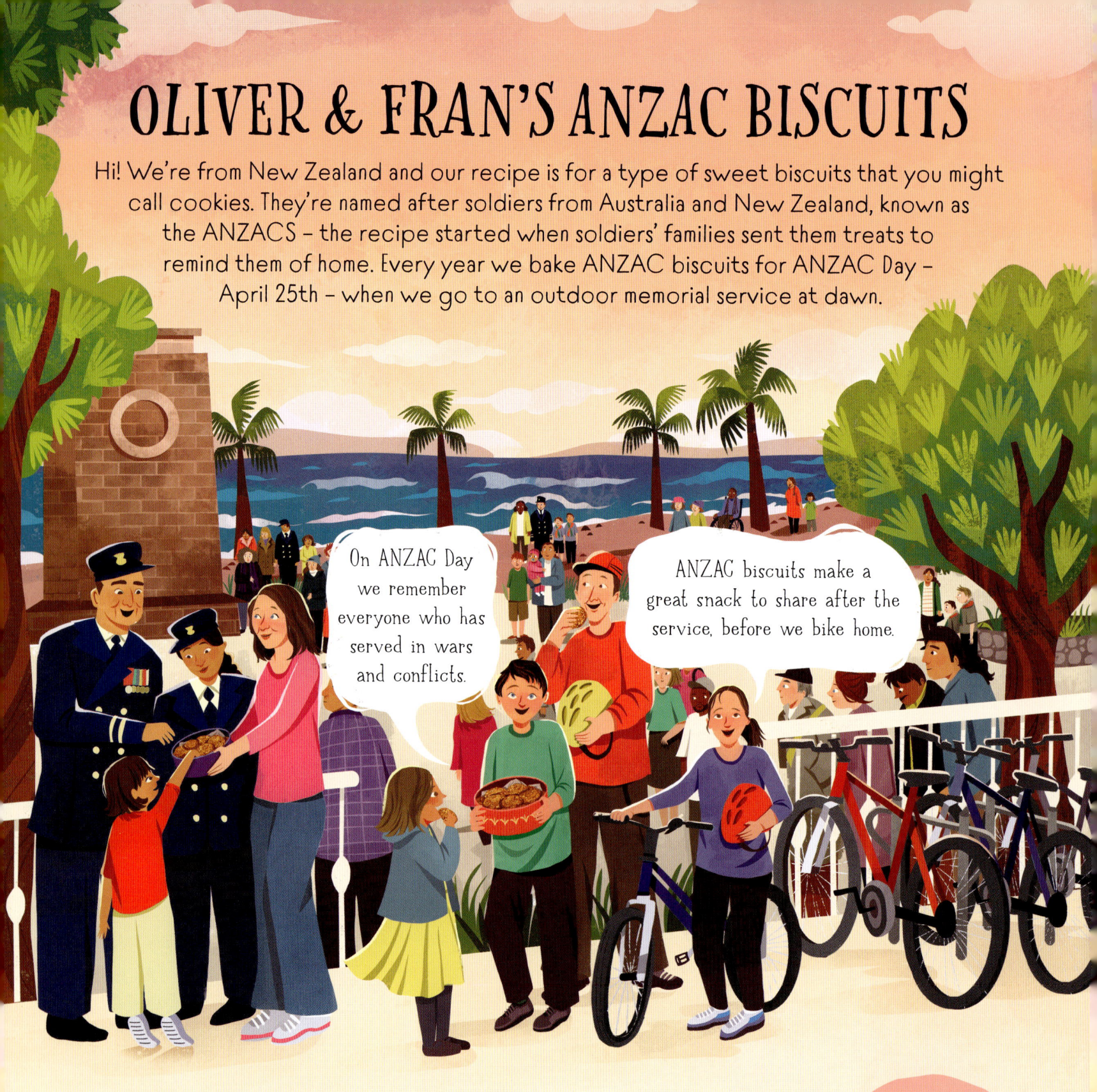

Hi! We're from New Zealand and our recipe is for a type of sweet biscuits that you might call cookies. They're named after soldiers from Australia and New Zealand, known as the ANZACS – the recipe started when soldiers' families sent them treats to remind them of home. Every year we bake ANZAC biscuits for ANZAC Day – April 25th – when we go to an outdoor memorial service at dawn.

On ANZAC Day we remember everyone who has served in wars and conflicts.

ANZAC biscuits make a great snack to share after the service, before we bike home.

INGREDIENTS

- 1 cup + 1 tablespoon all-purpose flour
- 1½ cups old-fashioned rolled oats
- ⅔ cup packed light brown sugar
- ½ cup unsweetened shredded coconut
- 9 tablespoons butter
- 2 tablespoons corn syrup
- 1 tablespoon water
- ½ teaspoon baking soda

You will also need two large baking sheets.

MAKES AROUND 25

1 Heat the oven to 350°F. Line the sheets with parchment paper.

The instructions on page 7 will show you how to do this.

2 Put the flour, oats, sugar and coconut in a big bowl.

Mix well.

3 Put the butter, corn syrup and water in a small pot over low heat.

Stir every now and then, until the butter melts.

4 Mix the baking soda into the butter mixture.

It will foam up!

5 Pour the butter mixture into the big bowl.

Mix everything together.

6 Scoop up a tablespoonful of the mixture.

Squash and roll it into a ball. Put it on a sheet.

7 Make more balls, until the mixture is used up.

Space them 1 inch apart, as they will spread out a lot.

8 If you like crispier biscuits, flatten the balls slightly.

If not, leave them round.

← Fork

9 Bake for 15-20 minutes, until golden-brown. Leave on the trays to cool.

They crisp up as they cool.

VARIATIONS

To make this recipe gluten-free, use gluten-free flour and gluten-free oats.

To make it dairy-free or vegan, replace the butter with plant-based "butter" from a block.

39

CELEBRATION DRINKS

A delicious soft drink can be part of a celebratory meal, or it may be enjoyed on its own as a festive treat. Either way, it's a wonderful (and sometimes fizzy, spiced or salty) way to mark a special occasion.

Home-made **LEMONADE** is a much-loved summer drink in the U.S. and Canada. This started when children made lemonade to sell to neighbors during their summer vacation. Now homemade lemonade is a favorite for summer parties.

You'll find a summery limeade recipe from Brazil on page 42.

A soft drink called **CHAPMAN** is a favorite for parties and get-togethers in Nigeria. It's a delicious mixture of lemonade, limeade and grenadine syrup (made from pomegranates) with a dash of bitter herb flavoring.

On page 54 you can find a recipe for fried rice that's also very popular at parties in Nigeria.

KOKO SAMOA, a hot chocolate drink, is very important in the island nation of Samoa. People often make it using chocolate grown on their own trees, and share it at important gatherings such as parties and weddings.

In Japan, **SAKURAYU** is tea made from pickled cherry blossoms. It's served hot, tastes slightly salty and is often shared at weddings.

A cold drink called **SORREL** is a central part of Christmas festivities in Caribbean countries. It's made by soaking parts of roselle (or hibiscus) flowers, and adding ginger and spices.

In the U.S. and Canada, **EGGNOG** is popular during the Christmas season. It's a thick, chilled drink made from milk, cream, sugar and eggs with a hint of cinnamon or nutmeg.

CHICHA MORADA is a bright purple drink from Peru, made by boiling purple corn with pineapple, quince and spices. It's popular in October, when people also wear purple for a religious procession in Lima, the capital of Peru.

41

MARILIA'S POOL PARTY LIMEADE

Hello! I'm Marilia and I'm from Brazil, where we love to party! My birthday is in the summer and as a child I always used to celebrate – and keep cool – with a pool party, and pitchers of iced limeade. I made it with my Vovô (Grandpa) using limes picked from our garden.

We always use a blender to make our limeade - but you can still make it if you don't have one.

INGREDIENTS

- 2 large limes, or 3 small limes
- ½ cup sugar
- 2½ cups cold water
- 3 tablespoons sweetened condensed milk
- ice, for serving

MAKES AROUND 4 GLASSES

1 Scrub the limes with a drop of dishwashing liquid, then rinse well.

Cut the limes into chunks.

2 If you have a blender or food processor, put in the lime chunks, sugar and water. Blend for a minute, until the chunks are in small pieces.

Pour it through a strainer into a wide pitcher. Then, skip to step 5.

3 If you don't have a blender or processor, cut the lime chunks into small pieces. Put them in a bowl with the sugar and water.

Stir well. Leave for 5 minutes.

4 Pour everything through a strainer into a wide pitcher.

Use the back of a spoon to press the lime pieces hard, to get out all the flavor.

5 Put the condensed milk and ice in the pitcher and stir well.

Pour into glasses, and enjoy!

Decorate the glasses with lime slices if you like.

VARIATIONS

For a dairy-free and vegan version, see the instructions on page 60.

PINTA'S RICE-FESTIVAL PANCAKES

Hi, my name is Pinta, and I come from the island of Sumatra, which is part of Indonesia. When I was growing up, my family made cimpa tuang – sweet rice and coconut pancakes. They are part of a festival called Kerja Tahun, to bring luck for the year's rice harvest.

INGREDIENTS

- ½ cup rice flour – if you can only get brown rice flour, see "Variations."
- 2 tablespoons palm sugar or light brown sugar
- 6 tablespoons coconut milk
- a pinch salt
- 2 teaspoons unsweetened shredded coconut
- a little cooking oil

We usually make big pancakes, but this recipe is for small ones as they're easier to flip.

MAKES AROUND 6

You will also need a large, non-stick frying pan.

1 Put the flour, sugar, coconut milk, salt and coconut in a big bowl.
Mix with a whisk.

2 Put a tablespoon of the oil in the pan. Put the pan over medium heat for 2 minutes. Turn the heat low. Drop in a tablespoon of the mixture.
Add 2 more tablespoons of the mixture, spaced well apart.

3 Cook for 3 minutes, until the edges are brown and a few bubbles appear.
Flip them over carefully. Cook for 2 more minutes.
Flexible spatulas

4 Put them on a plate. Cover with another plate.
Follow steps 2 and 3 again, until all the mixture is used up.

VARIATIONS

If you're using brown rice flour, follow the special instructions on page 60.

43

PAULA'S SHROVETIDE BUNS

Hi, my name is Paula and I come from Finland. As a child, I always looked forward to Shrovetide, a festival that falls in February or March, when the Finnish weather is still very cold and snowy. Finns celebrate by going sledding and eating rich food, including delicious cream buns delicately flavored with cardamom.

We always like to add jam to the whipped cream filling in our buns...

...other people prefer to use almond paste instead of jam – both are delicious!

INGREDIENTS

For the buns:
- 2 cups bread flour, plus extra for dusting
- 1 teaspoon (½ packet) fast-acting (instant) yeast
- 2 tablespoons sugar
- 1 teaspoon ground cardamom
- ¾ cup milk, plus a little extra for brushing
- 1 tablespoon cooking oil

For the filling:
- ⅔ cup heavy or whipping cream
- your favorite flavor of jam

MAKES 8

TIP
You'll need a warm place for the bun dough to rise – such as a warm radiator or sunny windowsill (with the window closed).

Or, turn your oven to the lowest temperature for 5 minutes, then turn it off and put the dough inside to rise.

44

1 Line a big baking sheet – see page 7 for instructions.

Mix the flour, yeast, sugar and cardamom in a big bowl.

2 Put the milk and oil in a pot over medium heat. After 2 minutes, test the temperature of the milk with the tip of a finger.

It should just feel warm – when it does, take it off the heat. Stir it into the flour mixture.

3 Sprinkle a surface with flour. Pour on the dough. If it's very sticky, sprinkle a little flour over it.

Knead the dough by pushing it away from you, using your knuckles or the heels of your hands.

4 Fold the dough in half towards you... ...then push it away again.

Keep doing this for 5-10 minutes, or until the dough is smooth and springy.

5 Put the dough back in the bowl. Put in a warm place for 1 hour, or until it's doubled in size.

Plate

6 Then, knead the dough again (see above) for 2 minutes.

Split it into 8 pieces. Roll into balls and put on the sheet. Put in a warm place for 30 minutes, or until doubled.

7 Next, heat the oven to 425°F.

Brush milk over the buns. Bake for 12 minutes, until golden-brown. Leave to cool on the sheet.

8 For the filling, pour the cream into a big bowl. Beat with a whisk or electric mixer.

The instructions on page 6 will help you.

9 Cut the tops off the buns, like this.

Spread 2 teaspoons of jam on each lower half. Top with whipped cream.

Then put the tops back on.

VARIATIONS

To make these buns gluten-free, use gluten-free white bread flour. At steps 4-6, knead for just a minute or two.

To make them dairy-free and vegan, use plant-based "milk" and plant-based whippable "cream."

45

BEN & ETHAN'S THANKSGIVING TARTS

Hi! We're brothers and we live in Canada. In October, we celebrate Thanksgiving – a time when we say thank you for all the good things we have. After a family meal at my Grandma's house, we eat these sweet tarts made with sugar, maple syrup and butter – they're called butter tarts. Then we go for a long walk – and finish up the butter tarts, if there are any left!

Sometimes we add raisins to our butter tarts – and sometimes we don't! You can choose.

MAKES 12

INGREDIENTS

For the pastry:
- 1½ cups + 2 tablespoons all-purpose flour
- ½ cup (1 stick) cold butter, plus extra for greasing
- ¼ cup cold water

You will also need a 12-hole deep muffin pan and a 4 inch round cutter.

For the filling:
- 6 tablespoons butter
- 1⅓ cup packed light brown sugar
- 4 tablespoons maple syrup
- 2 large eggs
- 1 teaspoon white wine vinegar
- 1 teaspoon vanilla extract
- ⅓ cup raisins (optional)

TIP
For the pastry, use cold butter from the refrigerator.

46

1 To make the pastry, put the flour in a big bowl.

Cut the butter into small cubes. Mix them in.

2 Pick up some butter and flour with the tips of your fingers and thumbs.

Squish and rub them together, letting the mixture drop into the bowl.

3 Keep on picking up the mixture, rubbing it and letting it fall.

The lumps of butter will get smaller. Stop when they are the size of peas.

4 Add the water. Use a blunt knife to mix it in gently.

Roll the pastry into a ball. Refrigerate for 30 minutes.

Plate → ← Bowl

5 Meanwhile, heat the oven to 350°F.

Rub a small chunk of butter all over the insides of the muffin pan.

6 To make the filling, put the butter in a small pot over gentle heat until it melts.

Put the butter in a measuring cup. Add the sugar and maple syrup.

7 Crack the eggs, following the instructions on page 6.

Pour the eggs into the cup. Add the vinegar and vanilla. Mix. This is the filling.

← Fork

8 Sprinkle a surface and rolling pin with flour. Roll out the pastry until it's half as thick as a pencil.

9 Use the cutter to cut lots of rounds. Press each round gently into a hole of the muffin pan.

Squeeze the scraps together, roll out again and cut more rounds, until the muffin pan is full.

10 Sprinkle some raisins into each pastry case.

Then pour in the filling. Each case should be almost full.

11 Bake for 20-25 minutes, or until the pastry is golden and the filling has puffed up.

Leave to cool completely. Then, lift the tarts out of the pan.

VARIATIONS

To make this recipe gluten-free, dairy-free, egg-free or vegan, follow the instructions on page 60.

47

ISHAQUE'S RAMADAN FRITTERS

Salaam! I'm Ishaque and my recipe is from Bangladesh, like my family. It's for eggplant fritters – delicious fried snacks. We make them during Ramadan – a time when people of the Muslim religion don't eat or drink during daylight hours. When the sun sets, we get together with family and friends and share water, dates and tasty snacks like these fritters.

We love spicy food, so we put chili powder and chili flakes in our fritters!

But if you prefer, you can leave out all the chili, or just use a small pinch.

1 Wash the eggplant, then cut it into round slices a little thinner than a pencil.

Throw away the top and bottom.

2 Arrange the slices on a clean dish cloth and sprinkle over the salt. Leave for 15 minutes.

This stops the eggplant from tasting bitter.

3 Prepare the potato (see page 6), then shred it. You will need ½ cup.

Grater

Big holes

4 Put the cilantro leaves and stalks in a cup. Snip them into small pieces.

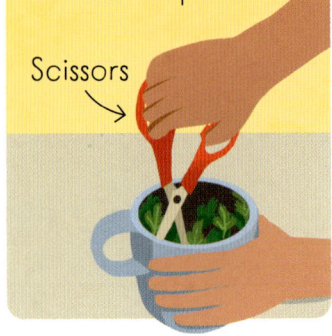

Scissors

5 Put the shredded potato, snipped cilantro, chickpea flour, chili flakes and chili powder in a big bowl.

Add the water and mix everything together.

6 Pat the eggplant slices dry with a clean dish cloth.

Put 2 tablespoons oil in the frying pan and put it over medium heat for 2 minutes.

INGREDIENTS

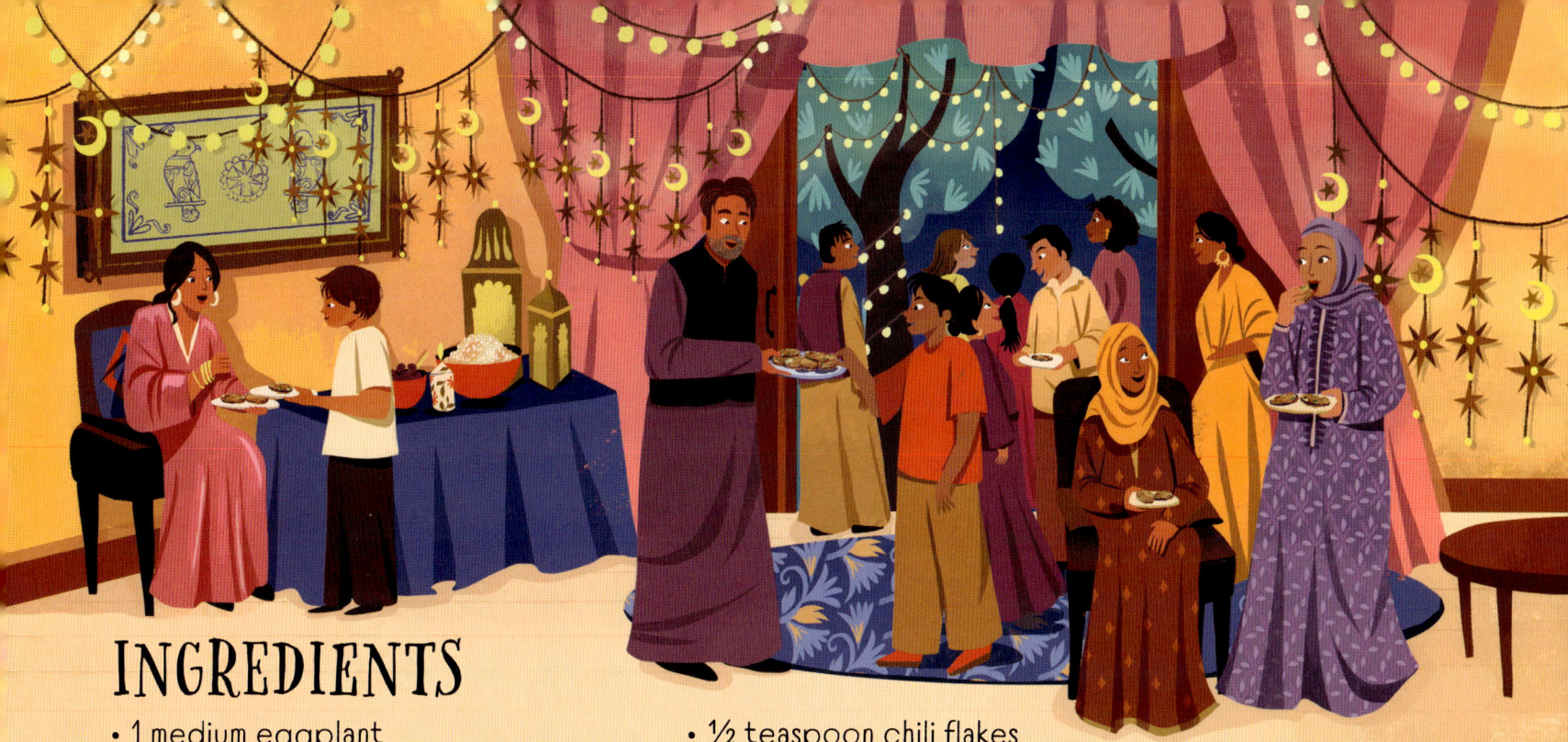

- 1 medium eggplant
- ½ teaspoon table salt
- 1 small potato (around 2oz)
- 3 stems of fresh cilantro leaves
- 1⅓ cups + 1 tablespoon chickpea flour
- ½ teaspoon chili flakes
- ½ teaspoon chili powder
- ¾ cup water
- a little cooking oil

You will also need a large frying pan, preferably non-stick.

7 Push an eggplant slice into the mixture so it's well coated on both sides.

Use tongs to pick it up and gently slide it into the frying pan.

8 Coat more slices and put them in the pan, leaving spaces between them. Cook for 5 minutes.

Use the tongs to turn them all over. Cook for 5 more minutes.

9 Line a plate with paper towels. Lift the fritters out of the pan and onto the plate. Cover with another plate.

Keep on coating and cooking, until you run out of eggplant or mixture.

10 Leave to cool for 10 minutes.

Eat while they're still warm, with ketchup, chili sauce or mint sauce.

VARIATIONS

This recipe is already gluten-free, nut-free, dairy-free, egg-free and vegan.

49

CELEBRATION HERBS & SPICES

For thousands of years, herbs and spices have been an essential part of recipes for feasts and festivals, providing beautiful colors, exciting flavors, and sometimes a kick of spicy heat!

A herb called **PANDAN** gives a sweet flavor and green color to many dishes from Vietnam, including banh bo nuong – a popular cake with a spongy texture that's enjoyed for festive occasions including Tê´t – Vietnamese Lunar New Year.

TURMERIC is a rich, yellow spice that's used in sfouf, a cake that's traditionally eaten in Lebanon for birthdays, family reunions and religious festivals.

CLOVES and **CINNAMON**, and sometimes other spices, are used to add a touch of spice to hot chocolate in Peru. There it's traditional to drink hot chocolate after Christmas dinner, which is eaten on December 24th.

50

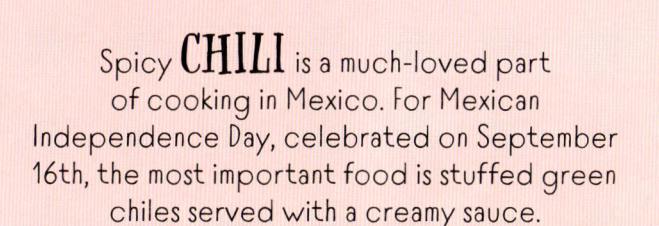

A spice called **SAFFRON** and other flavorings, including rose petals, are used to make javaher polow – jeweled rice. This dish is popular in Iran at weddings, engagements and other joyful occasions.

Spicy **CHILI** is a much-loved part of cooking in Mexico. For Mexican Independence Day, celebrated on September 16th, the most important food is stuffed green chiles served with a creamy sauce.

On page 26 you'll find a recipe from another country's Independence Day.

A spice called **CARDAMOM** is a key ingredient in a sweet rice pudding called "kheer" or "payasam." It's much loved in India, where it's served to people after they have taken part in services at Hindu temples.

GINGER is a favorite flavoring across Europe in cakes and cookies – such as Cornish Fairings. These are crisp, sweet ginger cookies from Cornwall, in the south of Britain. They were traditionally sold at fairs, where men used to buy them for their sweethearts as a sign of love.

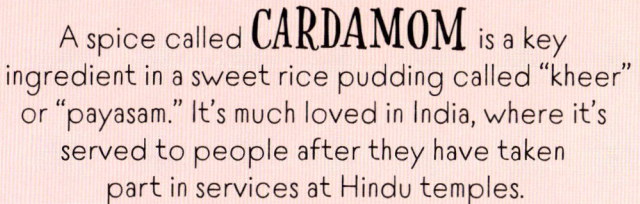

Cardamom is also used in the Finnish recipe on page 44.

51

TARA'S CELEBRATION CAKE

Hi! I'm Tara and I come from Guyana. When I was little, for special occasions I helped my Nanny (Grandmother) bake a cake so rich, moist and dark that it's called "black cake." It's made from dried fruits, spices and dark brown sugar. Before she baked it, Nanny soaked the fruit in rum for months – but you can soak your fruit in juice for just 30 minutes.

We baked this cake for a wedding, and covered it with marzipan and icing...

...but it's also delicious without icing, for any occasion!

INGREDIENTS

- 1 cup pitted prunes
- ⅓ cup glacé (candied) cherries
- 2½ cups mixed dried fruit (pitted)
- 1 cup chopped almonds (optional – leave out for anyone allergic to nuts)
- 1½ cups grape juice or prune juice
- ¾ cup (1½ sticks) butter
- 1 packed cup dark brown sugar
- 3 large eggs
- 1 teaspoon vanilla extract
- ½ teaspoon almond extract (optional – leave out for anyone allergic to nuts)
- 1 cup all-purpose flour
- 1 teaspoon baking powder
- ½ teaspoon ground cinnamon
- 1 teaspoon ground nutmeg
- ½ teaspoon ground cloves

You will also need an 8 inch springform cake pan.

TIP

Leave the butter and eggs at room temperature for 30 minutes before you start.

1. Snip the prunes and cherries into tiny pieces. Put them in a big bowl. Stir in the mixed dried fruit, almonds and juice. Leave to soak for 30 minutes.

2. Heat the oven to 300°F, then grease the sides and line the base of the pan. The instructions on page 7 will help you with this.

3. Put the butter and sugar in a big bowl. Mix really hard with a wooden spoon, until light and fluffy.

4. Crack an egg into a cup (see page 6). Then, mix it into the butter and sugar. Do this for each egg.

5. Stir in the vanilla and almond extract (if using). Then, stir in the flour, baking powder, cinnamon, nutmeg and cloves.

6. Pour in the soaked fruit and liquid. Stir well. Scrape it into the pan. Bake for 1½ hours.

7. Poke a toothpick into the middle. If it comes out clean, the cake is cooked. Mmm, smells amazing! If it has wet mixture on it, bake for 10 minutes more, then test again.

8. Leave the cake in the pan to cool completely. Then, run a knife between the cake and pan, unclip the pan and take off the sides.

9. Put an upside-down plate on top of the cake. Flip the cake and plate over together. Take off the base of the pan and peel off the paper.

10. Put an upside-down serving plate on the side of the cake facing up. Flip over the cake and both plates, then take off the top plate. Cut the cake into slices. Yum!

VARIATIONS

To make this recipe nut-free, leave out the almonds and almond extract.

To make it dairy-free, egg-free, vegan or gluten-free, follow the instructions on page 61.

53

OMOIHO'S PARTY RICE

Hello, my name is Omoiho and I come from Nigeria. My recipe is for delicious fried rice, flavored with coconut milk, colorful chopped vegetables, and a hint of curry powder. When I was a little girl, my Nene and Odede (Mother and Grandmother) always cooked this dish for my birthday parties – I loved it so much that I've been cooking it ever since.

We always use African brands of curry powder to flavor our rice...

...but it will still taste good with other types.

1 Put the rice in a bowl. Cover with cold water. Swirl, then drain in a strainer.

Cover, swirl and drain 2 more times. Put the rice in a shallow stockpot.

2 Pour 3 cups of the stock over the rice in the stockpot. Stir well.

Put the pot over medium heat. Wait until it starts to bubble.

3 When the liquid bubbles, turn down the heat so it bubbles gently. Put on a lid, leaving a gap. Cook for 10 minutes, stirring now and then.

Drain in a strainer, then rinse in cold water. Set aside.

4 Peel the papery skin off the onion and garlic. Crush the garlic. Cut the onion into small pieces.

The instructions on page 6 will help you.

5 Peel the carrot. Then cut both ends off the carrot, and off the beans.

Cut the carrot and beans into small pieces.

6 Prepare the bell peppers (see the instructions on page 7) then cut them into small pieces.

Snip both ends off the green onions. Snip the rest into small pieces.

INGREDIENTS

- 1½ cups instant long grain rice
- 3⅔ cups vegetable stock
- 1 medium onion
- 2 cloves garlic
- 1 medium carrot
- 2oz green beans
- ½ green bell pepper
- ½ red bell pepper
- 2 green onions
- 2 tablespoons coconut oil or vegetable oil
- ⅓ cup corn kernels from a can, or frozen
- 2½ teaspoons curry powder
- 1 teaspoon dried thyme
- 2 bay leaves
- 9 tablespoons coconut milk
- a pinch salt

You will also need a large non-stick pan.

7 Put the oil in the stockpot. Put it over medium heat for 2 minutes. Add the onion, carrot and beans.

Cook for 2 minutes, stirring now and then.

8 Add the garlic, peppers, the white parts of the green onions and the corn kernels.

Cook for 2 more minutes, stirring. Then stir in the curry powder, thyme and bay leaves.

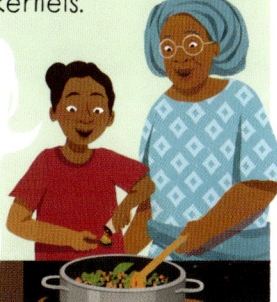

9 Pour the remaining ⅔ cup stock into the pan. Stir it in, then wait until it bubbles.

Pour the stock into the pan. Add the rice, coconut milk and salt.

10 Stir and put on a lid, leaving a small gap. Cook for 3 minutes.

Stir in the green parts of the spring onions. Cook for 2 more minutes. Pull out the bay leaves.

VARIATIONS

You can use mild, medium or hot curry powder in this recipe, depending on how spicy you like your food!

JAXON'S NEW YEAR PIE

Hello, I'm Jaxon. My Mom is from Bulgaria, and every New Year's Eve I help her to cook banitsa, a delicious Bulgarian pie made with lots of layers of crispy phyllo dough and a feta cheese filling. Banitsa is a much-loved dish in Bulgaria. We enjoy it hot or cold – we even eat it for breakfast sometimes!

For New Year banitsa, we write lucky events on slips of paper and tuck them under the pastry sheet...

...if you find a paper in your slice, you read it to discover your fortune for the New Year!

INGREDIENTS

- 6 tablespoons unsalted butter
- 2 large eggs
- 7oz feta cheese
- 2 tablespoons plain yogurt
- 1 package phyllo dough pastry sheets

You will also need a rectangular baking dish around 11 inches x 9 inches.

1 Heat the oven to 400°F. Put the butter in a small pot over low heat.

Wait until the butter melts. Then, set it aside.

2 Crack the eggs into a bowl – the instructions on page 6 will help you.

Beat the yolks and whites together.

← Fork

3 Crumble the feta into the bowl. Add the yogurt.

Mix well.

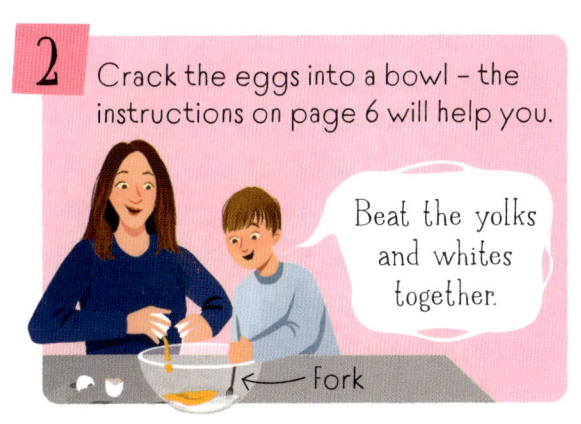

This is the filling.

4 Unroll the phyllo dough. Count the sheets. Put them into 3 piles with roughly equal numbers of sheets.

Brush some butter all over the inside of the baking dish.

5 Put in a phyllo dough sheet. If it's too big to fit flat in the dish, bunch it up.

Brush on some butter.

6 Put on another sheet and brush it with butter.

Do this until one pile of sheets is used up.

7 Spread on half the filling.

Cover it with more sheets brushed with butter, until another pile is used up.

8 Spread on the rest of the filling. Cover it with the last pile of phyllo dough sheets, brushing each with butter.

9 Score the top into squares, like this.

Sharp knife

10 Put a tablespoon of water in the bowl that held the filling. Swirl it around.

Brush it over the top. Leave for 5 minutes.

11 Bake for 12-15 minutes, or until the top is golden.

Leave to cool for 10 minutes, then cut into squares along the score lines.

VARIATIONS

To make this recipe gluten-free, dairy-free, egg-free or vegan, follow the instructions on page 61.

57

SWAPPING INGREDIENTS

All the recipes in this book are vegetarian, but you can make them vegan, nut-free, gluten-free, dairy-free, egg-free (or any combination of these) using the instructions that follow. If you're cooking for someone with special dietary requirements, always check packaged ingredients such as flour, cocoa powder, baking powder, spreads or sugar sprinkles, in case they contain anything unsuitable.

CARLY'S ST. DAVID'S DAY CAKES

- To make this recipe GLUTEN-FREE, use gluten-free self-rising flour and gluten-free baking powder.

JONATHAN'S HALLOWEEN COOKIES

- To make this recipe GLUTEN-FREE, use gluten-free flour and gluten-free baking powder.
- To make it DAIRY-FREE or VEGAN, use plant-based "butter" from a block and plant-based "milk."

GIORGIA'S NO-BAKE BIRTHDAY CAKE

- To make this recipe GLUTEN-FREE, use gluten-free graham crackers or vanilla wafers.
- To make it DAIRY-FREE or VEGAN, use plant-based chocolate, plant-based "butter" from a block, and plant-based "milk."

ARTHUR'S PASSOVER CHAROSET

- To make this recipe NUT-FREE, leave out the almond flour; instead you will need an additional ⅓ cup pitted dates. Before step 1, put these dates in a heatproof bowl, add ½ cup hot water and leave to soak for 15 minutes. Then, at step 3, drain them, chop them into tiny pieces and add them to the mixture in the bowl. Follow the rest of the steps as normal.

LARA'S TWELFTH NIGHT CAKE

- To make this recipe GLUTEN-FREE, use gluten-free puff pastry and gluten-free flour for sprinkling.
- To make it DAIRY-FREE, use plant-based puff pastry, use plant-based "butter" from a block and plant-based "milk" for brushing.
- To make it EGG-FREE, replace the egg with 2 tablespoons milk or plant-based "milk."
- To make it VEGAN, make it dairy-free and egg-free as above.
- To make it NUT-FREE, replace the almond flour with 3 cups fresh breadcrumbs – these can be gluten-free and/or plant-based if needed. To make fresh breadcrumbs from slices of bread, remove the crusts and crumble up the slices into crumbs.

BATOUL'S FAMILY-TIME SALAD

- To make this recipe PEANUT-FREE, replace the peanut butter with another type of nut butter such as almond or cashew.
- To make it NUT-FREE, replace the peanut butter with tahini (sesame seed paste – avoid this for anyone who can't eat sesame) or with soy-based peanut-free "peanut butter."

TOMOKO'S GIRLS' DAY SUSHI

- To make it EGG-FREE or VEGAN, leave out the eggs; instead, you will need a total of ¾ cup chickpea flour and 9 tablespoons water. After step 3, put ¼ cup chickpea flour in a bowl and whisk in 3 tablespoons of the water. Heat a little oil in a frying pan over medium heat. After 1 minute, pour in the mixture. Tilt the pan to spread it out. Cook for 2 minutes or until it all looks solid. Slide it out onto a plate. Repeat this process two more times, to make 3 "omelets" in total. Then follow the instructions in step 6 to cut them up. Follow the rest of the instructions as normal.

ELLIYA'S BARBADOS DAY CONKIES

- To make this recipe GLUTEN-FREE, use gluten-free flour.
- To make it DAIRY-FREE or VEGAN, use plant-based "milk" and plant-based "butter" from a block.

YVE'S CHRISTMAS EVE SALAD

- To make this recipe EGG-FREE or VEGAN, leave out the eggs and use plant-based "mayonnaise."

JOANNA'S DAY OF THE DEAD BREAD

- To make this recipe GLUTEN-FREE, use gluten-free bread flour.
- To make it DAIRY-FREE or VEGAN, use plant-based "butter" from a block and plant-based "milk."

ARACELI'S PALM SUNDAY TOAST

- To make this recipe GLUTEN-FREE, use gluten-free bread.
- To make it DAIRY-FREE, use plant-based "milk."
- To make it EGG-FREE, replace the egg with 4 tablespoons cornstarch or chickpea flour, and 4 tablespoons water, whisked together in a shallow bowl.
- To make it VEGAN, make it dairy-free and egg-free as above.

PINTA'S RICE-FESTIVAL PANCAKES

- This recipe is already vegan and free from gluten, dairy, egg and nuts.
- It's best to use rice flour made from white rice, because this gives the pancakes a smooth, firm texture. If you can only get brown rice flour, use just ⅓ cup of it and add 3½ tablespoons all-purpose flour, or gluten-free flour. This will make the pancakes smoother and firmer, and stop them from falling apart. Follow the steps as normal.

PAULA'S SHROVETIDE BUNS

- To make this recipe GLUTEN-FREE, use gluten-free white bread flour; at steps 4-6, knead for just a minute or two.
- To make it DAIRY-FREE and VEGAN, use plant-based "milk" and plant-based whippable "cream."

CHLOÉ'S NEW YEAR DUMPLINGS

- To make this recipe GLUTEN-FREE, use gluten-free bread flour.
- If you're avoiding sesame, use vegetable oil such as olive oil instead of the sesame oil.

OLIVER & FRAN'S ANZAC BISCUITS

- To make this recipe GLUTEN-FREE, use gluten-free self-rising flour and gluten-free oats.
- To make it DAIRY-FREE or VEGAN, replace the butter with plant-based "butter" from a block.

MARILIA'S POOL PARTY LIMEADE

- To make this recipe DAIRY-FREE or VEGAN, leave out the sweetened condensed milk; increase the amount of sugar to ½ cup + 1 tablespoon and at step 5 add 2½ tablespoons coconut milk.

BEN & ETHAN'S THANKSGIVING TARTS

- To make this recipe GLUTEN-FREE, replace the flour with gluten-free bread flour.
- To make it DAIRY-FREE, use plant-based "butter" from a block.
- To make it EGG-FREE, leave out the eggs and at step 7, mix 3 tablespoons of cornflour into the filling mixture instead.
- To make it VEGAN, make it dairy-free and egg-free as above.

ISHAQUE'S RAMADAN FRITTERS

- This recipe is already vegan and free from gluten, dairy, eggs and nuts.

TARA'S CELEBRATION CAKE

- To make this recipe GLUTEN-FREE, use gluten-free flour and gluten-free baking powder.
- To make it EGG-FREE, simply leave out the eggs.
- To make it DAIRY-FREE, use plant-based "butter" from a block.
- To make it VEGAN, make it egg-free and dairy-free as above.
- To make it NUT-FREE, leave out the almonds and almond extract.

OMOIHO'S PARTY RICE

- This recipe is already vegan and free from gluten, dairy, eggs and nuts.
- You can use mild, medium or hot curry powder, depending on how spicy you like your food.

JAXON'S NEW YEAR PIE

- To make this recipe GLUTEN-FREE, replace the phyllo dough with a package of gluten-free ready-rolled puff pastry, and replace the butter with 1 teaspoon vegetable oil. Skip the instructions in step 1 for melting the butter. At step 4, cut the puff pastry sheet in half; brush the oil all over the inside of the dish (instead of the butter). At step 5, line the bottom of the dish with one piece of the pastry. Put all the filling on top. Put the second piece of pastry on top. Skip steps 6, 7 and 8 and follow the remaining steps as usual.
- To make it EGG-FREE, leave out the eggs and at step 3, stir in 3 tablespoons cornstarch.
- To make it use DAIRY-FREE and VEGAN, use plant-based "butter" from a block and plant-based plain "yogurt;" leave out the feta cheese and at step 3, crumble 7oz firm tofu (1½ cups once crumbled) into the bowl, along with 3 tablespoons nutritional yeast and a pinch of salt and pepper. Follow the other instructions as normal.

61

INDEX

A
allergies, 4, 58-61
America, North, 23 (*see also* Canada *and* U.S.)
ANZAC,
   biscuits, 38-39, 60
   Day, 38
apples, preparing, 7
Araceli's Palm Sunday toast, 34-35, 59
Arthur's Passover charoset, 17, 58
Australia, 38
Bangladesh, 9, 48

B
Barbados Day conkies, 26-27, 59
Barbados, 8, 26
   Day, 26
Batoul's family-time salad, 20-21, 59
Belgium, 14,
Ben & Ethan's Thanksgiving tarts, 46-47, 60
birthdays, 15, 16, 42, 50, 54
   birthday cake, no-bake, 16, 58
biscuits, ANZAC, 38-39, 60
Brazil, 8, 33, 42
bread, Day of the Dead, 30-31, 59
Bulgaria, 9, 56
buns, Shrovetide, 44-45, 60

C
cakes,
   celebration, 14-15, 52-53, 61
   St. David's Day, 10-11, 58
   Tara's celebration, 52-53, 61
   Twelfth Night, 18-19, 58
Canada, 8, 14, 40, 41, 47
Caribbean, 41
Carly's St. David's Day cakes, 10-11, 58

celebration
   cake, Tara's, 52-53, 61
   cakes, 14-15
   drinks, 40-41
   fruits & vegetables, 22-23
   herbs & spices, 50-51
   sweets, 32-33
charoset, 17, 58
China, 14, 23
Chloé's New Year dumplings, 36-37, 60
chocolate, 16, 32, 33
Christianity, 32, 34
Christmas, 14, 18, 33, 41, 50
   Eve, 28
conkies, 26-27, 59
contents, 3
cookies, Jonathan's Halloween, 12-13, 58
cooking basics, 6-7
cream, whipping, 6, 44, 45

D
Day of the Dead, 30, 33
   bread, 30-31, 59
Diwali, 32
drinks, celebration, 40-41
dumplings, New Year, 36-37, 60

E
Easter, 32, 34
   eggs, 32
eggs,
   cracking, 6
   Easter, 32
Elliya's Barbados Day conkies, 26-27, 59
England, 15

F
family-time salad, 20-21, 59

Finland, 9, 44
France, 8, 14, 18
fritters, Ramadan, 48-49, 61
fruits & vegetables, celebration, 22-23

G
garlic, preparing, 6
Germany, 8, 28, 33
getting started, 4-5
Giorgia's no-bake birthday cake, 16, 58
Girls' Day, 24
Greece, 15, 33
Guyana, 8, 52

H
Halloween, 12, 23
   cookies, 12-13, 58
herbs & spices, celebration, 50-51
Hinduism, 51

I
Independence Day,
   Barbados, 26
   Mexico, 51
India, 14, 32, 51
Indonesia, 9, 14, 43
ingredients, swapping, 58-61
Iran, 33, 51
Ishaque's Ramadan fritters, 48-49, 61
Islam, 9, 23, 48
Italy, 8, 16, 32

J
Japan, 9, 24, 41
Jaxon's New Year pie, 56-57, 61
Judaism, 8, 17, 22

62

Joanna's Day of the Dead bread, 30-31, 59
Jonathan's Halloween cookies, 12-13, 58

K
kimchi, 36, 37

L
Lara's Twelfth Night cake, 18-19, 58
Lebanon, 50
limeade, 42, 60
lining pans and sheets, 7
Lunar New Year, 23, 36, 50

M
Malaysia, 14, 15, 23
map, 8-9
Marilia's pool party limeade, 42, 60
measuring, 4
Mexican Independence Day, 51
Mexico, 8, 30, 33, 51
Muslim, *see* Islam

N
New Year, 22, 23, 36, 50, 56
    dumplings, 36-37, 60
    Lunar, 23, 36, 50
    pie, 56-57, 61
New Zealand, 9, 38
Nigeria, 8, 40, 54
no-bake birthday cake, 16, 58
North America, 23 (*see also* Canada *and* U.S.)

O
Oliver & Fran's ANZAC biscuits, 38-39, 60
Omoiho's party rice, 54-55, 61
onions, preparing, 6
ovens, 5

P
Palm Sunday, 34
    toast, 34-35, 59
pancakes, rice-festival, 43, 60
pans, preparing, 7
parties, 40, 41, 54
    party rice, 54-55, 61
Passover, 9, 17
pastry, 18-19
    phyllo dough, 56, 57
Paula's Shrovetide buns, 44-45, 60
peppers, bell, preparing, 7
Peru, 41, 50
Philippines, the, 22, 23
pie, New Year, 56-57, 61
Pinta's rice-festival pancakes, 43, 60
pool party limeade, 42, 60
potatoes,
    potato salad, 28-29, 59
    preparing, 6
preparing ingredients, 6, 7

Q
Quicklinks, 2

R
Ramadan, 23, 48
    fritters, 48-49, 61
recipe map, 8-9
rice,
    party, 54-55, 61
    rice-festival pancakes, 43, 60

S
salad,
    Christmas Eve, 28-29, 59
    family-time, 20-21, 59
salt, 4
Samoa, 40
Seollal, 36
serving sizes, 4-5
Shrovetide, 44
    buns, 44-45, 60
Singapore, 14, 23
South Korea, 9, 36
Spain, 8, 34
St. David's Day, 10
Sudan, 9, 20
sushi, Girls' Day, 24-25, 59
swapping ingredients, 58-61
Sweden, 15
sweets, celebration, 32-33
Switzerland, 14, 22

T
Tara'a celebration cake, 52-53, 61
tarts, Thanksgiving, 46-47, 60
Thanksgiving, 46
    tarts, 46-47, 60
toast, Palm Sunday, 34-35, 59
Tomoko's Girls' Day sushi, 24-25, 59
Turkey, 33
Twelfth Night, 18
    cake, 18-19

U
U.S., 8, 12, 33, 40, 41

V
vegan substitutes, 58-61
Vietnam, 50

W
Wales, 8, 10
weddings, 33, 40, 41, 51, 52
whipping cream, 6

Y
Yve's Christmas Eve salad, 28-29, 59

ACKNOWLEDGEMENTS

Huge thanks to the following people and their families who have kindly given permission for their recipes to be included in this book.

ST. DAVID'S DAY CAKES, pages 10-11 – Carly Davies
HALLOWEEN COOKIES, pages 12-13 – Jody Lee
NO-BAKE BIRTHDAY CAKE, page 16 – Giorgia De Micheli
PASSOVER CHAROSET, page 17 – Susanna Davidson
TWELFTH NIGHT CAKE, pages 18-19 – Lara Bryan
FAMILY-TIME SALAD, pages 20-21 – Rawaa Elsir
GIRLS' DAY SUSHI, pages 24-25 – Tomoko Hori
BARBADOS DAY CONKIES, pages 26-27 – Linda Dudley & Jacqui Wiltshire
CHRISTMAS EVE SALAD, pages 28-29 – Yve McIntyre
DAY OF THE DEAD BREAD, pages 30-31 – Janet Castro
PALM SUNDAY TOAST, pages 34-35 – Araceli Garcia Navarro
NEW YEAR DUMPLINGS, pages 36-37 – Youngok Melmoth
ANZAC BISCUITS, pages 38-39 – Joanne Pascoe
POOL PARTY LIMEADE, page 42 – Marilia Abujamra
RICE-FESTIVAL PANCAKES, page 43 – Pinta Ulina Ginting
SHROVETIDE BUNS, pages 44-45 – Paula Ziedna
THANKSGIVING TARTS, pages 46-47 – Anthony Howard
RAMADAN FRITTERS, pages 48-49 – Nelupa Hussain
CELEBRATION CAKE, pages 52-53 – Tara Shah
PARTY RICE, pages 54-55 – Clara Omoiho Ogona
NEW YEAR PIE, pages 56-57 – Antonia Miller

SERIES EDITOR: Jane Chisholm   **SERIES DESIGNER:** Helen Lee
Additional design by Helen Cooke & Jamie Ball

First published in 2025 by Usborne Publishing Limited, 83-85 Saffron Hill, London EC1N 8RT, United Kingdom. usborne.com

Copyright © 2025 Usborne Publishing Limited. The name Usborne and the Balloon logo are registered trade marks of Usborne Publishing Limited. All rights reserved. No part of this publication may be reproduced or used in any manner for the purpose of training artificial intelligence technologies or systems (including for text or data mining), stored in retrieval systems or transmitted in any form or by any means without prior permission of the publisher. AE. First published in America 2025